**GRADES
5-6**

the Super Source™

Snap™ Cubes

Cuisenaire Company of America, Inc.
White Plains, NY

Cuisenaire extends its warmest thanks to the many teachers and students across the country who helped ensure the success of the Super Source™ series by participating in the outlining, writing, and field testing of the materials.

Project Director: Judith Adams
Managing Editor: Doris Hirschhorn
Editorial Team: John Nelson, Deborah J. Slade, Harriet Slonim, Linda Dodge, Patricia Kijak Anderson
Field Test Coordinator: Laurie Verdeschi

Design Manager: Phyllis Aycock
Text Design: Amy Berger, Tracey Munz
Line Art and Production: Joan Lee, Fiona Santoianni
Cover Design: Michael Muldoon
Illustrations: Jenny Williams

the Super Source™

Table of Contents

Using the Super Source™

The Super Source™ is a series of books each of which contains a collection of activities to use with a specific math manipulative. Driving the Super Source™ is Cuisenaire's conviction that children construct their own understandings through rich, hands-on mathematical experiences. Although the activities in each book are written for a specific grade range, they all connect to the core of mathematics learning that is important to every K-6 child. Thus, the material in many activities can easily be refocused for children at other grade levels. Because the activities are not arranged sequentially, children can work on any activity at any time.

The lessons in the Super Source™ all follow a basic structure consistent with the vision of mathematics teaching described in the Curriculum and Evaluation Standards for School Mathematics published by the National Council of Teachers of Mathematics.

All of the activities in this series involve Problem Solving, Communication, Reasoning, and Mathematical Connections—the first four NCTM Standards. Each activity also focuses on one or more of the following curriculum strands: Number, Geometry, Measurement, Patterns/Functions, Probability/Statistics, Logic.

HOW LESSONS ARE ORGANIZED

At the beginning of each lesson, you will find, to the right of the title, both the major curriculum strands to which the lesson relates and the particular topics that children will work with. Each lesson has three main sections. The first, GETTING READY, offers an Overview, which states what children will be doing, and why, and a list of "What You'll Need." Specific numbers of Snap Cubes are suggested on this list but can be adjusted as the needs of your specific situation dictate. Before an activity, cubes can be counted out and placed in containers of self-sealing plastic bags for easy distribution. If appropriate for an activity, the cubes might be distributed as color rods, 10 cubes per color. When crayons are called for, it is understood that their colors are those that match the Snap Cubes and that markers may be used in place of crayons. Blackline masters that are provided for your convenience at the back of the book are referenced on this list. Paper, pencils, scissors, tape, and materials for making charts, which are necessary in certain activities, are usually not.

Although overhead Snap Cubes are always listed in "What You'll Need" as optional, these materials are highly effective when you want to demonstrate the use of Snap Cubes. As you move the cubes on the screen, children can work with the same materials at their seats. Children can also use the overhead to present their work to other members of their group or to the class.

The second section, THE ACTIVITY, first presents a possible scenario for Introducing the children to the activity. The aim of this brief introduction is to help you give children the tools they will need to investigate independently. However, care has been taken to avoid undercutting the activity itself. Since these investigations are designed to enable children to increase their own mathematical power, the idea is to set the stage but not steal the show! The heart of the lesson, On Their Own, is found in a box at the top of the second page of each lesson. Here, rich problems stimulate many different problem-solving approaches and lead to a variety of solutions. These hands-on explorations have the potential for bringing children to new mathematical ideas and deepening skills.

On Their Own is intended as a stand-alone activity for children to explore with a partner or in a small group. Be sure to make the needed directions clearly visible. You may want to write them on the chalkboard or on an overhead or present them either on reusable cards or paper. For children who may have difficulty reading the directions, you can read them aloud or make sure that at least one "reader" is in each group.

The last part of this second section, *The Bigger Picture*, gives suggestions for how children can share their work and their thinking and make mathematical connections. Class charts and children's recorded work provide a springboard for discussion. Under "Thinking and Sharing," there are several prompts that you can use to promote discussion. Children will not be able to respond to these prompts with one-word answers. Instead, the prompts encourage children to describe what they notice, tell how they found their results and give the reasoning behind their answers. Thus children learn to verify their own results rather than relying on the teacher to determine if an answer is "right" or "wrong." Though the class discussion might immediately follow the investigation, it is important not to cut the activity short by having a class discussion too soon.

The Bigger Picture often includes a suggestion for a "Writing" (or drawing) assignment. This is meant to help children process what they have just been doing. You might want to use these ideas as a focus for daily or weekly entries in a math journal that each child keeps.

From: *Putting It All Together*

From: *Squares and Staircases*

The Bigger Picture always ends with ideas for "Extending the Activity." Extensions take the essence of the main activity and either alter or extend its parameters. These activities are well used with a class that becomes deeply involved in the primary activity or for children who finish before the others. In any case, it is probably a good idea to expose the entire class to the possibility of, and the results from, such extensions.

The third and final section of the lesson is TEACHER TALK. Here, in *Where's the Mathematics?*, you can gain insight into the underlying mathematics of the activity and discover some of the strategies children are apt to use as they work. Solutions are also given—when such are necessary and/or helpful. Because *Where's the Mathematics?* provides a view of what may happen in the lesson as well as the underlying mathematical potential that may grow out of it, this may be the section that you want to read before presenting the activity to children.

USING THE ACTIVITIES

The Super Source™ has been designed to fit into the variety of classroom environments in which it will be used. These range from a completely manipulative-based classroom to one in which manipulatives are just beginning to play a part. You may choose to use some activities in **the Super Source**™ in the way set forth in each lesson (introducing an activity to the whole class, then breaking the class up into groups that all work on the same task, and so forth). You will then be able to circulate among the groups as they work to observe and perhaps comment on each child's work. This approach requires a full classroom set of materials but allows you to concentrate on the variety of ways that children respond to a given activity.

Alternatively, you may wish to make two or three related activities available to different groups of children at the same time. You may even wish to use different manipulatives to explore the same mathematical concept. (Cuisenaire® Rods and Color Tiles, for example, can be used to teach some of the same concepts as Snap Cubes.) This approach does not require full classroom sets of a particular manipulative. It also permits greater adaptation of materials to individual children's needs and/or preferences.

If children are comfortable working independently, you might want to set up a "menu"— that is, set out a number of related activities from which children can choose. Children should be encouraged to write about their experiences with these independent activities.

However you choose to use **the Super Source**™ activities, it would be wise to allow time for several groups or the entire class to share their experiences. The dynamics of this type of interaction, in which children share not only solutions and strategies but also feelings and intuitions, is the basis of continued mathematical growth. It allows children who are beginning to form a mathematical structure to clarify it and those who have mastered just isolated concepts to begin to see how these concepts might fit together.

Again, both the individual teaching style and combined learning styles of the children should dictate the specific method of utilizing **the Super Source**™ lessons. At first sight, some activities may appear too difficult for some of your children, and you may find yourself tempted to actually "teach" by modeling exactly how an activity can lead to a particular learning outcome. If you do this, you rob children of the chance to try the activity in whatever way they can. As long as children have a way to begin an investigation, give them time and opportunity to see it through. Instead of making assumptions about what children will or won't do, watch and listen. The excitement and challenge of the activity—as well as the chance to work cooperatively—may bring out abilities in children that will surprise you.

If you are convinced, however, that an activity does not suit your students, adjust it, by all means. You may want to change the language, either by simplifying it or by referring to specific vocabulary that you and your children already use and are comfortable with. On the other hand, if you suspect that an activity is not challenging enough, you may want to read through the activity extensions for a variation that you can give children instead.

RECORDING

Although the direct process of working with Snap Cubes is a valuable one, it is afterward, when children look at, compare, share, and think about their constructions, that an activity yields its greatest rewards. However, because Snap Cube designs can't always be left intact, children need an effective way to record their work. To this end, at the back of this book recording paper is provided for reproduction. The "What You'll Need" listing at the beginning of each lesson often specifies the kind of recording paper to use. For example, it seems natural for children to record Snap Cube patterns on grid paper. Yet it is important for children to use a method of recording that they feel comfortable with. Frustration in recording their structures can leave children feeling that the actual activity was either too difficult or just not fun! Thus, there may be times when you feel children should just share their work rather than record it.

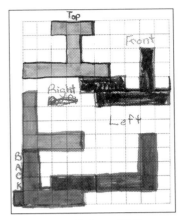

From: *Point of View*

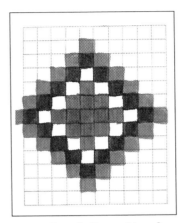

From: *Greek Cross Numbers*

Young children might duplicate their work on grid paper by coloring in boxes on grids that exactly match the cubes in size. Older children may be able to use smaller grids or even construct the recording paper as they see fit.

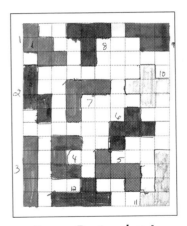

From: *Pentacubes I*

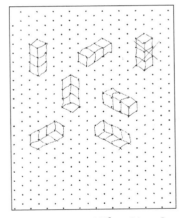

From: *Draw What You See*

Another type of recording paper, isometric dot paper, can also be introduced for recording three-dimensional Snap Cube constructions. As they become more familiar with isometric dot paper, children begin to see that they can represent a corner of a cube by a dot on paper and that they now have a method of communicating visually about three-dimensional objects.

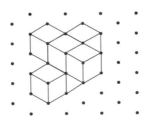

Another interesting way to "freeze" a Snap Cube design is to create it using a software piece, such as *Building Perspective*, and then get a printout. Children can use a classroom or resource-room computer if it is available or, where possible, extend the activity into a home assignment by utilizing their home computers.

Recording involves more than copying structures. Writing, drawing, and making charts and tables are also ways to record. By creating a table of data gathered in the course of their investigations, children are able to draw conclusions and look for patterns. When children write or draw, either in their group or later by themselves, they are clarifying their understanding of their recent mathematical experience.

From: *Triangular Number Sequence*

	number of cubes					
	0	1	2	3	4 or more	Total
Round 1	13	14	7	0	2	36
Round 2	18	12	2	3	1	36
Round 3	20	5	0	6	5	36
Total	51	31	9	9	8	108

From: *What's the Chance?*

Stories	Amount Added	Total Cubes
1	1	1
2	3	4
3	5	9
4	7	16
5	9	25
6	11	36
10	19	100
99	197	9801
100	199	10000

From: *Squares and Staircases*

4.   16

                                            8
                                            64

Key
◼ 8 "set of cubes
◼ 8 stories
□ total cubes

5. 21 stories high because 20 on each side and 1 in the middle would work out as a base of 41 perfectly.

6. I thought there would be few blocks. Around 1000, but it turns out the total number of blocks equals 10,000.

From: *Squares and Staircases*

With a roomful of children busily engaged in their investigations, it is not easy for a teacher to keep track of how individual children are working. Having tangible material to gather and examine when the time is right will help you to keep in close touch with each child's learning.

Exploring Snap™ Cubes

Snap Cubes are a versatile collection of three-quarter-inch interlocking cubes which come in ten colors and connect on all six sides. They are pleasant to handle, easy to manipulate and, although simple in concept, can be used to develop a wide variety of mathematical ideas at many different levels of complexity. Since Snap Cubes come in ten different colors, the cubes are useful for developing patterns, both one- and two-dimensional, based on color. The cubes can be arranged in a single layer to naturally fit into a square grid pattern, or they can be used to cover positions on a printed grid or game board. When the cubes are used to build three-dimensional structures, they lead naturally to the concepts of volume and surface area.

> ① You will need 6 blues, 11 whites, 11 reds
> ② Put the 6 blues together to form a rectangle.
> ③ Put 4 reds in a line.
> ④ Put 4 whites in a line.
> ⑤ Then put 7 reds in a line
> ⑥ Then put 7 whites in a line.
> ⑦ Now put them together to form a rectangle that you will recognise.

From: *Putting It All Together*

The colors of the Snap Cubes can also be used to identify cubes in other contexts. For example, the different colors can represent designated quantities in various number situations. They become a sampling device when they are drawn from a bag, and they aid in concretely building bar graphs.

> 1. No, we did not. Yes, we did. Yes, we did.
> 2. Yes, they did because they kept landing on the same box and that was not our prediction.
> 3. Our classmates' answers were very similar to ours.
> 4. It would be 2/36.
> 5. A seven would be a greater probability.

From: *What's the Chance?*

WORKING WITH SNAP™ CUBES

Snap Cubes make natural and appealing counters. Since they snap together firmly, they are useful for young children as number models. If children build a stick corresponding to each number from 1 to 10, it is natural for them to arrange them in a staircase and to talk about greater and less, longer and shorter. Numbers might also be represented by the following cube patterns, which are easily sorted into "even" ones, in which each cube is paired with another, and "odd" ones, in which there is an "odd man out."

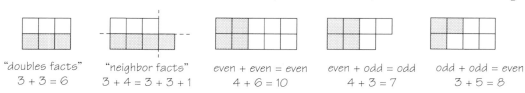

Snap Cubes also help children to more easily see relationships such as the following:

"doubles facts"	"neighbor facts"	even + even = even	even + odd = odd	odd + odd = even
3 + 3 = 6	3 + 4 = 3 + 3 + 1	4 + 6 = 10	4 + 3 = 7	3 + 5 = 8

Since there are large numbers of cubes in a set of Snap Cubes, they are useful for estimation and for developing number sense. Children can make a long rod with the cubes, estimate how many there are in the rod, and then separate the rod into sticks of 10, identify how many tens they have, and count the "leftovers" to find how many ones there are.

The colors of the cubes further make them useful in developing the concept of place value. Each color can represent a place value, and children can play exchange games in which if they have 10 of one color they can exchange them for one of the next color.

Snap Cubes are very suitable for developing understanding of the meaning of addition. They can be used as loose counters, with a different color for each addend. The colors can also broaden children's understanding of subtraction. Children often think initially of subtraction as "take away." To act out 6 – 4, children put out 6 cubes and take away 4.

Snap Cubes are also ideal for developing the concept of multiplication, both as grouping and as an array. To show 3 x 4, children can make 3 "cube trains" with 4 in each and count them all. Arranging these cubes in a rectangular array not only makes it visually easy to understand why 3 x 4 = 4 x 3 but also leads naturally into a model for understanding the formula for the area of a rectangle. In addition, Snap Cubes are suitable for exploring area, perimeter, volume, and surface area relations.

> ① Master Builder because you just build anything while the Apprentice has to listen to the builder and build what he describes.

From: *Master Builder*

Snap Cubes are a wonderful tool to use in helping children to represent numbers in terms of factors and to understand procedures of finding greatest common divisors and least common multiples. Snap Cubes are also a natural unit for length, and using them can lead to early experience of ratio and proportion. Children can measure the same length in Snap Cubes and in another unit, perhaps inches. They can record their results for a few different lengths. They may then measure in just one unit and predict the measure in the other.

ASSESSING CHILDREN'S UNDERSTANDING

Snap Cubes are wonderful tools for assessing children's mathematical thinking. Watching children work on their Snap Cubes gives you a sense of how they approach a mathematical problem. Their thinking can be "seen," in so far as that thinking is expressed through the way they construct, recognize, and continue spatial patterns. When a class breaks up into small working groups, you are able to circulate, listen, and raise questions, all the while focusing on how individuals are thinking. Here is a perfect opportunity for authentic assessment.

Having children describe their structures and share their strategies and thinking with the whole class gives you another opportunity for observational assessment. Furthermore, you may want to gather children's recorded work or invite them to choose pieces to add to their math portfolios.

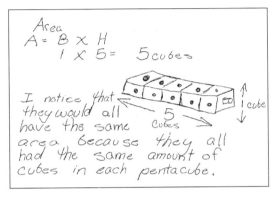

Area
A = B × H
1 × 5 = 5 cubes

I notice that they would all have the same area because they all had the same amount of cubes in each pentacube.

From: *Pentacubes I*

1. The number 108 could appear in the column labeled 2 faces. The reason it could be put in 2 faces column is because the 2 faces column consists of multiplying by 12.

From: *Painted Cubes*

Models of teachers assessing children's understanding can be found in Cuisenaire's series of videotapes listed below. Snap Cubes can be used in many of the lessons shown on the *Color Tiles* and *Six Models* tapes.

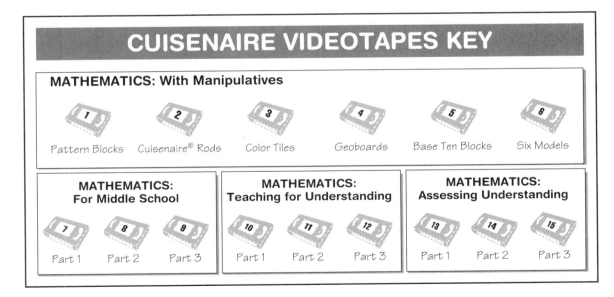

CUISENAIRE VIDEOTAPES KEY

MATHEMATICS: With Manipulatives

1	*2*	*3*	*4*	*5*	*6*
Pattern Blocks	Cuisenaire® Rods	Color Tiles	Geoboards	Base Ten Blocks	Six Models

MATHEMATICS: For Middle School			MATHEMATICS: Teaching for Understanding			MATHEMATICS: Assessing Understanding		
7	*8*	*9*	*10*	*11*	*12*	*13*	*14*	*15*
Part 1	Part 2	Part 3	Part 1	Part 2	Part 3	Part 1	Part 2	Part 3

	PROBLEM SOLVING	COMMUNICATION	REASONING	CONNECTIONS	Geometry	Logic	Measurement	Number	Patterns/Functions	Probability/Statistics
DRAW WHAT YOU SEE	♦	♦	♦	♦	♦					
END OF MY ROPE	♦	♦	♦	♦	♦			♦		
FRAC-TANGLES	♦	♦	♦					♦		
GREEK CROSS NUMBERS	♦	♦	♦	♦				♦	♦	
MASTER BUILDER	♦	♦	♦	♦	♦	♦				
MATCH/NO MATCH	♦	♦	♦	♦						♦
MYSTERY GRIDS	♦	♦	♦			♦				
PAINTED CUBES	♦	♦	♦	♦	♦				♦	
PENTACUBES I	♦	♦	♦	♦	♦	♦				
PENTACUBES II	♦	♦	♦	♦	♦	♦				
PENTA NETS	♦	♦	♦	♦	♦					
POINT OF VIEW	♦	♦	♦	♦	♦					
PUTTING IT ALL TOGETHER	♦	♦	♦	♦	♦	♦				
PYRAMID NUMBERS	♦	♦	♦	♦				♦	♦	
SQUARES AND STAIRCASES	♦	♦	♦	♦				♦	♦	
SURFACE AREA WITH 12 CUBES	♦	♦	♦	♦	♦		♦			
TRIANGULAR NUMBER SEQUENCE	♦	♦	♦	♦				♦	♦	
WHAT'S THE CHANCE?	♦	♦	♦	♦						♦

TOPICS

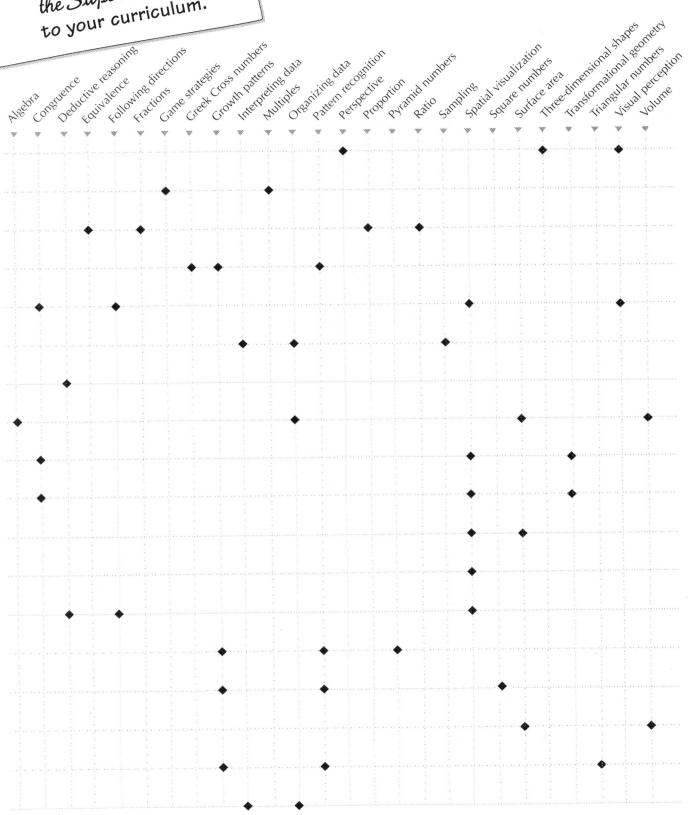

Algebra · Congruence · Deductive reasoning · Equivalence · Following directions · Fractions · Game strategies · Greek Cross numbers · Growth patterns · Interpreting data · Multiples · Organizing data · Pattern recognition · Perspective · Proportion · Pyramid numbers · Ratio · Sampling · Spatial visualization · Square numbers · Surface area · Three-dimensional shapes · Transformational geometry · Triangular numbers · Visual perception · Volume

Classroom-tested activities contained in these *Super Source*™ Snap™ Cubes books focus on the math strands in the charts below.

the Super Source™ **Snap™ Cubes, Grades K-2**

Geometry	Logic	Measurement
Number	Patterns/Functions	Probability/Statistics

the Super Source™ **Snap™ Cubes, Grades 3-4**

Geometry	Logic	Measurement
Number	Patterns/Functions	Probability/Statistics

More SUPER SOURCE™ at a glance:
ADDITIONAL MANIPULATIVES for Grades 5-6

Classroom-tested activities contained in these *Super Source™* books focus on the math strands as indicated in these charts.

the Super Source™ Tangrams, Grades 5-6

Geometry	Logic	Measurement
Number	Patterns/Functions	Probability/Statistics

the Super Source™ Cuisenaire® Rods, Grades 5-6

Geometry	Logic	Measurement
Number	Patterns/Functions	Probability/Statistics

the Super Source™ Geoboards, Grades 5-6

Geometry	Logic	Measurement
Number	Patterns/Functions	Probability/Statistics

the Super Source™ Color Tiles, Grades 5-6

Geometry	Logic	Measurement
Number	Patterns/Functions	Probability/Statistics

the Super Source™ Pattern Blocks, Grades 5-6

Geometry	Logic	Measurement
Number	Patterns/Functions	Probability/Statistics

Overview of the Lessons

Snap™ Cubes, Grades 5-6

DRAW WHAT YOU SEE

- **Three-dimensional shapes**
- **Perspective**
- **Visual perception**

Getting Ready

What You'll Need

Snap Cubes, 3 per child

Isometric dot paper, 1 sheet per child, page 90

Overhead isometric dot paper transparency (optional)

Overview

Children build a train of Snap Cubes, look at it from various angles, and then use isometric dot paper to record what they see. In this activity, children have the opportunity to:

- ◆ focus on visual perspective
- ◆ represent three-dimensional objects in a two-dimensional plane
- ◆ use isometric dot paper as a mathematical tool

The Activity

Let children know that while isometric dot paper is helpful when drawing three-dimensional objects in perspective, using it takes practice and can sometimes be frustrating.

Introducing

- ◆ Have each child place a Snap Cube on a flat surface and turn it so that three sides are visible. Ask children how many corners, or vertices, they can see.

- ◆ Translate what children see in three dimensions into a two-dimensional drawing on isometric paper. Shade the top face.

- ◆ Point out that the seven dots in the drawing match the seven corners that children can see on their cubes.

- ◆ Connect another set of seven dots and shade the bottom face. Ask children to hold the cube in the position that shows what this drawing represents.

On Their Own

Can you draw all the different views of a 3-cube Snap Cube train?

- Make a train of 3 Snap Cubes.

- Use isometric dot paper to draw as many different views of the train as you can.

- Each view should show 3 sides of the train.

- Compare your results with those of other members of your group.

- Be ready to talk about how your drawings show 3 dimensions.

The Bigger Picture

Thinking and Sharing

Have volunteers take turns sharing the solutions until all six solutions are shown. You may want to suggest that children draw solutions on an isometric dot paper transparency which you can then display on the overhead projector. Have children hold up their cubes in the positions that match each two-dimensional solution.

Use prompts such as these to promote class discussion:

- What did you discover about drawing trains?

- Why are there only six dot-paper drawings for the three-cube train?

- What was difficult about the activity? What was easy? Why?

- In what real-world situations might isometric dot paper be useful?

Writing

Have children make a list of tips for drawing three-dimensional objects in two dimensions that can be used by someone who is just learning to work with isometric dot paper.

Extending the Activity

1. Ask children to construct a Snap Cube building. Then, tell them to make three or four different isometric dot paper drawings of their building. Have children exchange only their drawings with a partner and use them to try to build each other's structures.

2. Have children use isometric dot paper to discover the 24 possible perspective drawings of a five-cube T-shaped structure. This would be a good long-term class project.

Where's the Mathematics?

Being able to draw in perspective is crucial to communicating about three-dimensional objects. By using isometric dot paper, children can record their views of three-dimensional objects in two dimensions. Children can represent each visible corner of a cube by a dot on the paper.

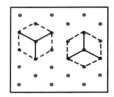

In the *Introducing*, children may have thought that there would be six—or even eight—different drawings possible because they know a cube has six faces and eight corners. Yet every drawing that shows perspective can be recorded in only two ways.

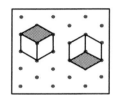

As they draw the different perspectives of their train, children may need to move their train so that the corners of the cubes are positioned to match the dots on the isometric paper. The lines that they draw will then represent the edges of the Snap Cubes.

By investigating different views of the train, children may realize that not all of the views can be or need to be drawn on isometric dot paper. For example, when viewing one of the square faces straight on, the representation could only look like this:

When viewing one of the rectangular faces straight on, the representation could only look like this:

Only six different isometric drawings of the train are possible.

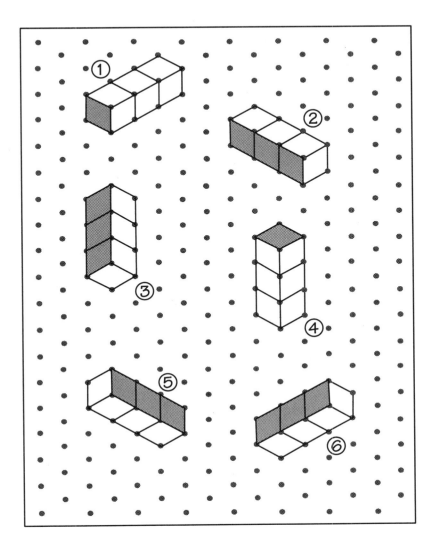

With experience, children discover the fun of communicating visually about objects in space. As they experiment, children begin to grasp the connection between a three-dimensional object and its representation on isometric dot paper. The aspect of perspective may not be evident to children when manipulating the cubes. Eventually, however, most children will notice that parallel edges of a rectangular prism are represented by parallel lines on the paper and the square faces are represented by rhombuses. They will also realize that shading enhances their drawings.

END OF MY ROPE

Getting Ready

What You'll Need

Snap Cubes, 21 per pair

Overhead Snap Cubes and/or Snap Cube grid paper transparency (optional)

Overview

Children play a game in which they take turns removing one, two, or three cubes from a cube "rope." They develop strategies to avoid taking the last cube and losing the game. In this activity, children have the opportunity to:

◆ use deductive reasoning

◆ develop strategic thinking skills

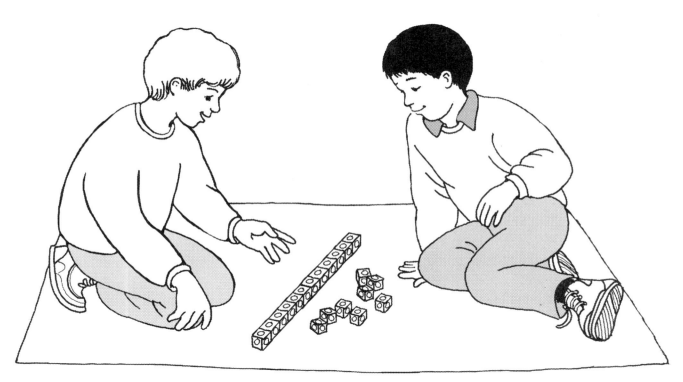

The Activity

Introducing

◆ Tell children that they will be working to design a winning strategy for a Snap Cube game.

◆ Point out that Tic-Tac-Toe is an example of a game of strategy.

◆ Invite a volunteer who thinks he or she has a good Tic-Tac-Toe strategy to come to the chalkboard and play against you.

◆ After the game is over, ask the volunteer to explain his or her strategy.

◆ Ask children to share other strategies that might be useful. You may wish to play a few more games at the board.

On Their Own

Play *End of My Rope!*

Here are the rules.

1. This is a game for 2 players. The object of the game is to make the other player remove the last Snap Cube.

2. Players make a "rope" of 21 Snap Cubes.

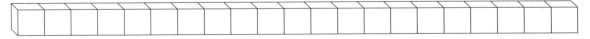

3. Players take turns removing 1, 2, or 3 cubes at a time. No player may skip a turn.

4. The player who takes the last cube "runs out of rope" and loses the game.

- Play 5 games of *End of My Rope*.

- Be ready to talk about good moves and bad moves.

The Bigger Picture

Thinking and Sharing

Ask volunteers to describe a strategy they used. Encourage all children to try the described strategy and test whether or not it works. Allow them to play the game a few more times after the class discussion to validate the winning strategies.

Use prompts such as these to promote class discussion:

- What did you find out about how to play this game?

- Does it matter who goes first? Why do you think that?

- On a turn, how did you decide whether to take one, two, or three cubes?

- Did you ever try copying your opponent's move? What happened?

Writing

Have children explain the best way to win the *End of My Rope* game.

Extending the Activity

1. Have children play *End of My Rope* again, this time making a rope with more than 21 Snap Cubes.

2. Have children play the game again, making the player who removes the last cube the winner.

Where's the Mathematics?

This game helps children develop, analyze, and compare strategies designed to produce a given outcome in a game situation. Developing a winning strategy is analogous to the scientific process: Children start by playing the game with no particular strategy in mind. They begin to see patterns and formulate ideas about how to win. This is the inductive stage in which children make observations and suggest hypotheses. They test the game theory and may have to refine it and test it again before they are satisfied at having found a winning strategy. Finally, if children can go back over the strategy and propose logical reasons for why it is a winning strategy, they have succeeded.

At first, most children will try a relatively random strategy. For example, they may explain that to win, "You should play any number until there are fewer than 10 left and then play very carefully." Others may test strategies that sound systematic, but are not based on an analysis of the situation. Examples of this type of strategy are copying what the other player does or thinking that the first person to play is always the winner or the loser. Some children will develop a strategy, test it successfully once, and be convinced that it will always work. Children need to be encouraged to see that one success is not always enough to judge the validity of a strategy. As children describe their strategies, they should explain how they arrived at them.

What is most important in this activity is developing the ability to evaluate a situation and think ahead to predict the consequences of a particular action. If children claim that they "can't think of any strategy," suggest that they set their cubes aside in the order in which they removed them so they can study that pattern to help them formulate a strategy. One child can place his or her removed cubes above the "rope" and the other child can place his or her removed cubes below the rope. This will help them record the action of each turn.

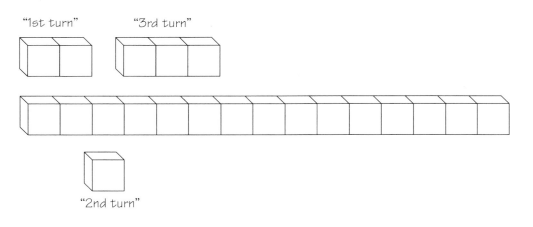

Some children will have difficulty articulating what they are thinking. Others will be able to explain their winning strategy but may be unable to accept that another person has expressed a similar idea in different words. Playing the game again after changing the rules is a good way to help children to learn how to generalize as they adapt their winning strategy to a new situation.

One winning strategy is to think of the 21 Snap Cubes as five groups of 4 cubes and one group of 1 cube. Here are the cubes, grouped and numbered.

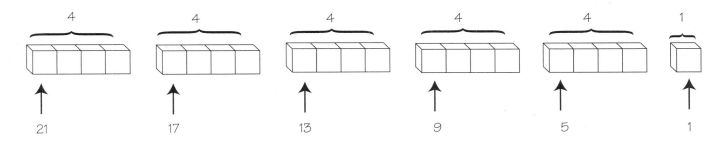

Since a player can remove only 1, 2, or 3 cubes at a time, each complete turn (Player A and Player B taking cubes) can be held to a sum of 4 cubes removed; that is, if Player A takes 1, Player B takes 3; if Player A takes 2, Player B takes 2; if Player A takes 3, Player B takes 1. The player who uses the sum-of-4 strategy can win if the other player is left with 17, 13, 9, or 5 out of the 21 cubes. Thus, the player who goes second can always win. If the first player can manage to leave the second player with 17, 13, 9, or 5 cubes on the rope, then that player can take control of the game and use the sum-of-4 strategy to win.

FRAC-TANGLES

- **Fractions**
- **Ratio**
- **Equivalence**
- **Proportion**

Getting Ready

What You'll Need

Snap Cubes, 40 in a mixture of colors per child

Snap Cube grid paper, page 91

Crayons

Overhead Snap Cubes and/or Snap Cube grid paper transparency (optional)

Overview

Using Snap Cubes, children make rectangular prisms from clues given about the fractional mix of colors. In this activity, children have the opportunity to:

- ◆ discover that there are many ways to show the same fraction
- ◆ develop strategies for showing fractions using geometry and tables
- ◆ use ratio and proportion

The Activity

You may wish to write

$$\frac{number\ of\ yellow\ cubes}{total\ number\ of\ cubes}$$

to help children see that the denominator of the fraction is not just the blue cubes but rather all the cubes in the rectangle.

Introducing

- ◆ Show children a rectangle made of one yellow cube and two blue cubes. Ask them what fraction of the rectangle is yellow.
- ◆ Ask children to use their Snap Cubes to build a rectangle that is one third of one color and two thirds of another color and uses more than three cubes.
- ◆ Have volunteers share their rectangles with the class and explain how they know they have satisfied the requirement that one third of the cubes are color A and the rest of the cubes are color B. Ask them how many cubes of color A they used and how many cubes they used in the rectangle. Write these numbers as a fraction. Here are some examples:

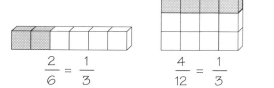

$$\frac{2}{6} = \frac{1}{3} \qquad \frac{4}{12} = \frac{1}{3} \qquad \frac{3}{9} = \frac{1}{3}$$

- ◆ Establish that many rectangles are possible.

On Their Own

> ### How many Snap Cube rectangles can you make that satisfy these Frac-tangle puzzles?
>
> - Work with a partner to solve each Frac-tangle puzzle.
>
> - Use Snap Cubes to build a rectangle that satisfies the clues in the puzzle. Find as many different solutions as you can. One solution is different from another if it requires a different number of Snap Cubes to make the rectangle or if the dimensions of the rectangle are different.
>
>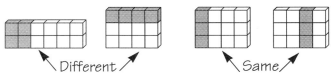
>
> - When you have found a solution, copy it onto grid paper and color the grid to show the solution. Look for patterns if there are multiple solutions.
>
> #### Frac-tangle Puzzles
>
> *Frac-tangle #1*
> This rectangle is ½ blue and ¼ yellow. The rest of the rectangle is black.
>
> *Frac-tangle #2*
> This rectangle has 12 cubes. Three of the cubes are green. One fourth of them are red. One sixth of them are yellow, and the rest are blue.
>
> *Frac-tangle #3*
> This rectangle is ⅜ blue and ¼ yellow. The rest of the rectangle is red.
>
> *Frac-tangle #4*
> This rectangle is ⅗ red. The rest is blue and yellow but not in equal amounts.

The Bigger Picture

Thinking and Sharing

Discuss each puzzle. Have several pairs present their solutions. Place solutions for each Frac-tangle in a table to help children see patterns. Make a class chart showing the number and color of cubes in each Frac-tangle.

Use prompts like these to promote class discussion:

- How did you go about solving this problem?
- How many solutions did this puzzle have?
- What patterns do you notice?
- How can you tell that this rectangle shows _____ (name fraction)?
- When you say that (give a fraction, such as ⁴⁄₁₂) are yellow, what do the 4 and 12 represent in the rectangle? Why is ⁴⁄₁₂ another name for ⅓?

Extending the Activity

Have children create their own Frac-tangle puzzle, then exchange puzzles and find the solutions.

Where's the Mathematics?

Frac-tangles 1, 3, and 4 do not specify the total number of cubes in the rectangle, so they have multiple solutions for the mix of colors as well as for the dimensions of the rectangles. For Frac-tangle 1, some children will reason that ¼ of the cubes are black since ½ are blue and ¼ are yellow. If they realize that ½ is twice as large as ¼, they will know that for every yellow or black cube they use, they must have 2 blue cubes.

Children who use a trial-and-error approach may find the patterns in the class chart helpful. For example, if children had found the only two solutions and put them in the table like the one below, they may see that the numbers in the second column are 4 times as large as the ones in the first column and this may lead them to experiment with multiplying by different numbers and to find other solutions. No matter which two columns of numbers children find, juxtapositioning them often reveals a pattern.

Number of blue cubes	2	8
Number of yellow cubes	1	4
Number of black cubes	1	4
Total number of cubes	4	16

Here are solutions for Frac-tangles 3 and 4:

Frac-tangle #3

Blue cubes	3	6	9	12	15	18	...
Yellow cubes	2	4	6	8	10	12	...
Red cubes	3	6	9	12	15	18	...
Total cubes	8	16	24	32	40	48	...

Frac-tangle #4

Red cubes	6	12	18	24	30	36	...
Blue cubes	1	2	3	4	5	6	...
Yellow cubes	3	6	9	12	15	18	...
Total cubes	10	20	30	40	50	60	...

Since Frac-tangle 4 states that the blue and yellow are not in equal amounts, the row of numbers in the *Blue Cubes* row of the table could be interchanged with the row of numbers in the *Yellow Cubes* row.

These tables help point out the multiples that are used to form equivalent fractions. Any two rows can be pulled out to create a series of equivalent fractions. For example, from the rows for the number of blue cubes and the total number of cubes for Frac-tangle 4, these fractions result:

$$\frac{1}{10} = \frac{2}{20} = \frac{3}{30} = \frac{4}{40} = \frac{5}{50} = \frac{6}{60} = \dots$$

Frac-tangle 2 is the only puzzle with exactly one solution as far as the number of each colored cube is concerned, although children will find rectangles with 3 different dimensions: 1 x 12, 2 x 6, and 3 x 4. This puzzle is different from the others because the total number of cubes is given. Some children may use arithmetic to figure out that ¼ of 12 means 3 red cubes and ⅙ of 12 means 2 yellow cubes. Since it is given that there are 3 green cubes, they can use subtraction to figure out that 12 – 3 – 2 – 3 leaves 4 blue cubes. If children are not familiar with arithmetic operations with fractions, they will probably use a trial-and-error approach to solve the problem.

When asked to explain what the 4 and 12 in the fraction ⁴⁄₁₂ mean, children should be able to explain that the 4 refers to the number of yellow cubes in the rectangle and the 12 refers to the total number of cubes in the rectangle. When asked to explain why ⁴⁄₁₂ is equivalent to ⅓, some children may break the cubes into 4 groups of one yellow and two other colored cubes and explain that one out of every three cubes is yellow. Other children may separate the 12 cubes showing a group of 4 yellow and two groups of 4 comprised of colors other than yellow, and then explain that one out of every three groups is yellow.

Manipulating a less recognizable form of the fraction into something that looks more familiar will help deepen children's understanding of the concept of what a fraction means. After their experiences with these puzzles, children may be more accepting of a wide variety of fractional representations.

GREEK CROSS NUMBERS

- Greek Cross numbers
- Pattern recognition
- Growth patterns

Getting Ready

What You'll Need

Snap Cubes, at least 45 per pair

Calculators, 1 per pair

Snap Cube grid paper, page 91 (optional)

Crayons (optional)

Overhead Snap Cubes and/or Snap Cube grid paper transparency (optional)

Overview

Using Snap Cubes, children build models of Greek Cross numbers. They record data about each structure, look for patterns, and make conjectures. In this activity, children have the opportunity to:

- ◆ represent a numerical sequence geometrically
- ◆ collect and analyze data
- ◆ learn about a predictable growth pattern
- ◆ use patterns to make predictions

Activity

Some children may predict that four, instead of eight, cubes should be added, thinking that the new structure looks like this.

Point out that this cannot be a solution, since the cubes surrounding the middle cube are covered on only two, not four, sides.

Introducing

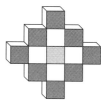

- ◆ Display one Snap Cube. Then cover two pairs of opposite sides with cubes of another color.

- ◆ Display the new structure. Ask children to predict how many cubes will be needed to cover all but a pair of opposite sides of every exposed Snap Cube. Then, using cubes of a third color, make your structure look like the one shown.

- ◆ Count the cubes to confirm that eight were needed.

- ◆ Explain that the number of cubes contained in the structures you made—1, 5, and 13—are called *Greek Cross numbers*. They are so named because the structures look like crosses and Greek mathematicians were the first to study the structure of numbers in depth.

On Their Own

Is there a way to know in advance the number of Snap Cubes you would need and how to connect them in order to build a Greek Cross structure of any size?

- Work with a partner to build Greek Cross structures that look like this:

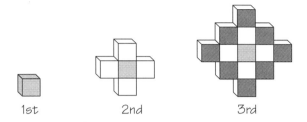

1st   2nd   3rd

- Keep track of the number of cubes you add each time, the total number of cubes in each Greek Cross, and the patterns you find.

- Predict what the 4th structure will look like, then build it.

- Build structures until you can use your findings to describe, in detail, the 10th Greek Cross structure without building it.

The Bigger Picture

Thinking and Sharing

Create a class chart with three columns. Label the first column *Greek Cross Number*, the second column *Number of Cubes Added*, and the third column, *Total Number of Cubes*. Have children fill in the chart and discuss the data.

Use prompts like these to promote class discussion:

- What did you notice as you built bigger and bigger Greek Cross structures?
- What patterns do you notice in the data?
- How many structures did you need to build before you could make predictions about the tenth Greek Cross? Why?
- How did you find the number of cubes needed for the tenth Greek Cross?
- How is the tenth Greek Cross different from the ninth Greek Cross? from the eleventh Greek Cross?

If children have done Triangular Number Sequence *and* Squares and Staircases, *have them take out their work from those activities to compare to findings in this activity.*

Writing

Ask children to describe the fifteenth Greek Cross number and explain their thinking.

Extending the Activity

Have children graph their data. On one graph, the numbers along the horizontal axis can represent the "Greek Cross Number" and the number along the vertical axis can represent the "Number of Cubes Added." On a second

Where's the Mathematics?

The first ten Greek Cross numbers appear in the third column of the class chart, shown below. The second column contains consecutive multiples of four. The first column contains counting numbers. All three number sequences grow in predictable ways.

Greek Cross Number	Number of Cubes Added	Total Number of Cubes
1	0	1
2	4	5
3	8	13
4	12	25
5	16	41
6	20	61
7	24	85
8	28	113
9	32	145
10	36	181

After building three or four Greek Cross structures, children start to notice patterns. They may see the symmetry of the structures, both line and rotational. From a bird's eye view, they may notice that each new structure is formed by adding cubes in multiples of four. For example, the second Greek Cross can be thought of as 1 + 4, the third Greek Cross as 1 + 4 + 8, and the fourth as 1 + 4 + 8 + 12. Children may suggest that the number of cubes added is always the structure number minus 1 times 4, that is, Greek Cross 5 has (5 – 1) x 4, or 16, more cubes than Greek Cross 4.

Children may also think of each structure as rows of consecutive odd numbers. For instance, Greek Cross 2 has two odd numbers of cubes: 1 + 3 + 1. The Greek Cross 3 has three odd numbers of cubes: 1 + 3 + 5 + 3 + 1.

graph, have children change the vertical axis so it represents the "Total Number of Cubes." Have children compare graphs.

Furthermore, the number of rows (or columns) is always the Greek Cross number doubled less 1. Thus, Greek Cross 3 has (2 x 3) – 1, or 5, rows; Greek Cross 4 has (2 x 4) – 1, or 7, rows. The doubling occurs because of the symmetry of the structure and the need to subtract 1 occurs because there is only one longest row. In fact, the number of rows (or columns) always describes the number of cubes in the longest row (or column). Thus, the longest row in Greek Cross 3, which consists of 5 rows, has 5 cubes.

Some children may point out that each Greek Cross can be separated into two staircases made of consecutive square numbers of cubes. For example, the taller staircase in Greek Cross 3 has 3^2, or 9, cubes and the shorter staircase has 2^2, or 4, cubes, for a total of 13 cubes. Continuing this pattern, it is possible to predict the following without building each structure: Greek Cross 4 has $4^2 + 3^2$, or 25, cubes, Greek Cross 5 has $5^2 + 4^2$, or 41, cubes, and Greek Cross 6 has $6^2 + 5^2$, or 61, cubes.

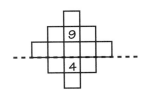

Each Greek Cross can also be visualized as part of a square array in which the total number of cubes in the Greek Cross is a square number minus four times a triangular number. For example, Greek Cross 3 fits into a 5-by-5 square, as shown, since its longest row has 5 cubes. Each of the remaining pairs have 3 and 1 cubes, respectively. This leaves 3 cubes in each corner that are not part of the Greek Cross. Thus, (5 x 5) – (4 x 3) gives a total of 13 cubes.

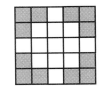

Using the patterns found in the structures and on the chart, the tenth Greek Cross number must have (2 x 10) –1, or 19, rows. Its longest row must have 19 cubes. Each row has an odd number of cubes, thus, the structure must look like this: 1 + 3 + 5 + 7 + 9 + 11 + 13 + 15 + 17 + 19 + 17 + 15 + 13 + 11 + 9 + 7 + 5 + 3 + 1. And, the total number of cubes needed is 181. Two other approaches will confirm this sum. One is using increasing multiples of 4, that is finding the sum of 1 + 4 + 8 + 12 + 16 + 20 + 24 + 32 + 36. The other is using a square array, that is $19^2 – (4 \times 45)$.

MASTER BUILDER

- Spatial visualization
- Following directions
- Congruence
- Visual perception

Getting Ready

What You'll Need

Snap Cubes, 12 of 1 color per child
Books or heavy folders to use
as barriers

Overview

Children build a structure with Snap Cubes, keep it hidden from view, and then describe the structure in such a way that their partner will be able to build an identical structure. In this activity, children have the opportunity to:

- ◆ use precise language to describe geometric attributes and spatial relationships
- ◆ improve their listening and visualization skills
- ◆ practice using effective questioning techniques

The Activity

Introducing

- ◆ Build a Snap Cube structure similar to the one shown at the right.
- ◆ Ask children to imagine that they are on the telephone with their best friend and they are trying to instruct their friend on how to build an identical structure. Ask volunteers for some helpful ways to describe this structure so that the friend at the other end of the telephone would be able to build the structure.
- ◆ List the descriptions on the chalkboard. Accept all reasonable descriptions. Encourage class discussion of descriptions that children find questionable.

On Their Own

> **Can you describe your Snap Cube structure so that someone else could build a structure that is exactly the same as yours?**
>
> - Work with a partner. Decide who will be the Architect and who will be the Master Builder. Set up a barrier so neither of you can see the other's workspace.
>
> - The Architect uses 8 to 12 Snap Cubes to build a structure. Then the Architect describes the structure to the Master Builder.
>
> - The Master Builder listens to the description and tries to build a structure that exactly matches the Architect's. The Master Builder may not ask any questions.
>
> - When the Master Builder is finished, remove the barrier. Decide if the structures are exactly the same. If they are not, discuss why.
>
> - Repeat the activity, but this time, the Master Builder may ask questions.
>
> - Switch roles and try the activity again.

The Bigger Picture

Thinking and Sharing

After partners have each had at least two turns at being the Master Builder, ask children to describe what happened during the activity. Invite volunteers to discuss how successful they were in building matching structures.

Use prompts such as these to promote class discussion:

- Was it easier to be the Master Builder or the Architect? Why?

- Did it make a difference when the Master Builder was allowed to ask questions? Explain.

- What kinds of things were hardest to describe? What kinds of things were easiest to describe?

- Were there any mathematical words that you found to be useful in your descriptions or questions? Which ones?

- What tips would you give to an Architect? to a Master Builder?

- If you did the activity again, what would you do differently?

Writing

Ask children to tell about which they would rather be—the Architect or the Master Builder—and to explain their choice.

Extending the Activity

1. Ask children to repeat the activity with this change: The Master Builder may ask only *yes* or *no* questions.

Where's the Mathematics?

This activity of creating precise descriptions can help children strengthen their spatial reasoning skills as they convey information about a three-dimensional object through a verbal description. Children frequently find that a word or phrase can mean different things to different people. For example, when directed to place a cube "on top of" an existing 2-by-2 square, some children may build upward into a third dimension while others may extend the structure by adding to its length or width.

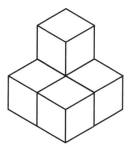 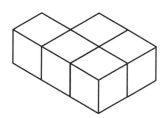

As children work through this activity, they gain an awareness of the necessity of establishing a common understanding to clarify terms that may be open to interpretation—terms such as *above, left, below, next to, between,* and *adjacent.*

The opportunity to use mathematical language in context is crucial in the construction of mathematical understanding. Mathematical terms such as *face, edge, adjacent, parallel, perpendicular, between,* and *diagonal* provide children with the means to give a more precise description of the structure. It is a good idea to keep a running list of mathematical terms on a large chart for all to see and refer to. This list should be compiled as the terms emerge in context and become part of the dialogue. In this way, a word is connected to an experience, helping to make discussion of the term meaningful. In addition, a picture or diagram drawn next to some terms on the list provides a good visual reference.

Children should recognize that the goal of the Architect is not to try to trick the Master Builder, but rather to provide useful descriptions that will enable the Master Builder to build an exact replica of the structure. *Master Builder* is not a competitive game. The importance of the skills brought to the task by *both* partners—describing, listening, visualizing, and later, questioning—

You may want to have children write their own definitions of the terms. This process can give insight into the level of understanding that children have attained. It also provides children with the opportunity to clarify and develop their thinking through the process of writing.

2. Have children work with their partners to build a structure and write a set of directions that could be used to build it. Have children exchange directions with another team and try to build each other's structures.

becomes more and more evident as children repeat the activity and take turns at the two roles.

In comparing the two structures, children have an opportunity to deepen their understanding of congruence. They need to scrutinize their structures carefully to determine whether or not they are identical. Since the Master Builder's structure must be congruent to the Architect's, children may need to change the orientation of the structures by flipping and rotating them. Structures that are mirror images, such as the ones pictured below, are not congruent.

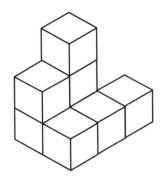 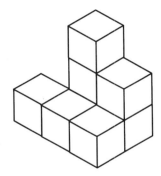

The task of comparing structures provides immediate feedback for the partners on how well they were able to communicate with each other. Children can figure out what descriptions may have been misinterpreted and discuss better ways of explaining or describing those particular attributes of the structures.

Some children may be frustrated by the rule that prohibits them from asking questions. This initial restriction helps children to focus on the information they need and on the value of forming good questions to get that information. Later, when children are allowed to add questioning to the activity, they may have acquired a sense of the kinds of questions that will provide the most useful information.

The ability to use precise language and follow directions comes with practice. Once children have acquired this skill, they will have a greater chance of succeeding not just in mathematics, but in any academic discipline that involves communications.

MATCH/ NO MATCH

- Organizing data
- Interpreting data
- Sampling

Getting Ready

What You'll Need

Snap Cubes, 4 red and 7 blue (or 4 and 7 of any other two colors) per pair

Brown paper lunch bags, 3 per pair

Overview

Children use Snap Cubes to play a game with three variations and determine which variation is fair. In this activity, children have the opportunity to:

- ◆ collect and analyze data
- ◆ learn about sampling and sample size
- ◆ see the difference between experimental (or empirical) and theoretical probability
- ◆ discover the meaning of equally likely outcomes

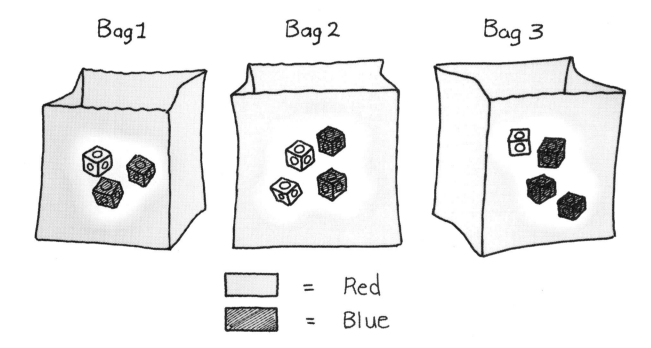

Bag 1   Bag 2   Bag 3

▭ = Red

▨ = Blue

The Activity

Introducing

- ◆ Ask children to think of their favorite games. Make a list.
- ◆ Ask children if they think these games are fair and why.
- ◆ Explain that mathematicians consider a game fair if each player has the same chance of winning or if each possible outcome has the same chance of happening.

On Their Own

Play *Match/No Match!*

Here are the rules.

1. This is a game for 2 players. The object is to be the player who gets more points as a result of drawing matching or non-matching Snap Cubes from a bag.

2. Players label and fill a set of 3 *Match/No Match* bags as follows:

   Bag 1: 1 red Snap Cube and 2 blue Snap Cubes
   Bag 2: 2 red Snap Cubes and 2 blue Snap Cubes
   Bag 3: 1 red Snap Cube and 3 blue Snap Cubes

3. Players read the game rules and predict which bag(s) will make *Match/No Match* a fair game. Then play *Match/No Match* using Bag 1.

4. Players decide who is Player A and who is Player B.

5. Each player draws a cube from Bag 1, without looking.

6. If the colors match, Player A wins a point. If the colors don't match, Player B wins a point. Players record the score.

7. Players put the cubes back in the bag, shake the bag, and draw again. They repeat this 20 times.

8. The player with more points after 20 draws wins.

9. Compare the results of playing with Bag 1 to your prediction.

- Play the game again using Bag 2. Then play using Bag 3.
- Be ready to explain which of the bags will make the game fair.

The Bigger Picture

Thinking and Sharing

Have children record their results for Bag 1 on a class chart that looks like the one to the right. Do the same for Bag 2 and Bag 3. Discuss which bags seems fair and why.

Use prompts like these to promote class discussion:

Bag 1	
Match	No Match
6	14
5	15
•	•
•	•
•	•

- Did your results match your prediction?
- Did the class results match your prediction?
- Does the class data match your data? Explain.
- On the class chart, how many times did Player A win? Player B?
- What fraction of the games did Player A win? Player B?
- What does the class data indicate?
- Are any of the bags fair for the game of *Match/No Match*? Explain.

Writing

Have children write about their *Match/No Match* experiences by explaining why each bag was fair or unfair.

Teacher Talk

Where's the Mathematics?

This sampling activity gives children the opportunity to see the relationship between the theoretical data and experimental (empirical) data. Most children will be surprised that Bag 3 is the bag that makes *Match/No Match* a fair game. Intuition might indicate that Bag 2 is the fair one since it has equal numbers of colors and most children would associate the equal numbers with fairness. In fact, a limited number of samples may support this intuition. The taking of multiple samples and combining the results of the whole class, however, will show that the number of matches and non-matches are most nearly the same for Bag 3. In other words, the fairness of Bag 3 becomes apparent only after a large number of games have been played.

Theoretically, in order for a game such as *Match/No Match* to be fair, both players have to have an equally likely chance of winning. That means that the number of possible match outcomes must equal the possible number of no-match outcomes.

Tree diagrams, lists, and matrices provide ways to find out whether one outcome is as likely theoretically to happen as another. To analyze the outcomes, cubes of the same color must be distinguished from each other. In this tree diagram for Bag 1, B1 and B2 represent the two blue cubes and R1 represents the red cube. The tree diagram indicates the six possible outcomes, two that are matches and four that are not. The game would be unfair with Bag 1 since the probability of a match is $\frac{2}{6}$ or $\frac{1}{3}$ and the probability of a non-match is $\frac{4}{6}$ or $\frac{2}{3}$.

Bag 1 Outcomes

```
            B 2   (match)
     B 1 <
            R 1   (no match)

            B 1   (match)
     B 2 <
            R 1   (no match)

            B 1   (no match)
     R 1 <
            B 2   (no match)
```

Extending the Activity

Have children invent their own *Match/No Match* game using three colors of Snap Cubes. Then have them analyze their game for fairness.

Some children prefer to list the possible outcomes instead of making a tree diagram. Since each cube in Bag 2 can be paired with three other cubes, there are 12 possible outcomes. These outcomes are:

Bag 2 Outcomes

B1, B2 (match)   B2, B1 (match)
B1, R1 (no match)   B2, R1 (no match)
B1, R2 (no match)   B2, R2 (no match)

R1, B1 (no match)   R2, B1 (no match)
R1, B2 (no match)   R2, B2 (no match)
R1, R2 (match)   R2, R1 (match)

The list shows that there are four ways to make a match. Therefore, the probability of a match is $\frac{4}{12}$ or $\frac{2}{6}$ or $\frac{1}{3}$. Likewise, the probability of a non-match is $\frac{8}{12}$ or $\frac{4}{6}$ or $\frac{2}{3}$.

A third way to analyze possible outcomes is with a matrix—a grid in which each cube in the bag is listed once along the top and once down the side. Here is a matrix showing the outcomes for Bag 3.

Bag 3 Outcomes

	B1	R1	R2	R3
B1	X	B1R1	B1R2	B1R3
R1	R1B1	X	(R1R2)	(R1R3)
R2	R2B1	(R2R1)	X	(R2R3)
R3	R3B1	(R3R1)	(R3R2)	X

The X's in the grid represent the four impossible outcomes. For example, once a cube is drawn from the bag by Player A, it cannot be picked by Player B. The matches are circled, indicating that probability of a match is 6 out of 12 or $\frac{1}{2}$. Since the same probability exists for a non-match, Bag 3 is the only fair bag.

MYSTERY GRIDS

Getting Ready

What You'll Need

Snap Cubes, 3 each of 3 different colors per child

Snap Cube grid paper, 1 sheet per child, page 91 (optional)

Overhead Snap Cubes and/or Snap Cube grid paper transparency (optional)

Overview

In this game for two players, one player tries to guess the secret Snap Cube arrangement created by the opposing player. In this activity, children have the opportunity to:

◆ develop deductive reasoning skills

◆ visualize flips and rotations

The Activity

Children might describe the arrangement shown in the following ways:

"Each row has 3 different colors in it."

"All the cubes in one of the diagonals are the same color."

"The top cube in the second column is green."

"A blue cube is in the top right corner. It is next to (adjacent to) two green cubes and a red cube touches its edge."

Introducing

◆ Hold up a cube and identify its parts as *face*, *edge*, and *vertex*.

◆ Ask children to snap together nine Snap Cubes to form a 3-by-3 arrangement.

◆ Have children think of all the ways to describe their arrangements.

◆ Invite several volunteers, one at a time, to share their arrangements and their descriptions.

◆ Establish the meaning of the terms *row*, *column*, *diagonal*, and *adjacent*.

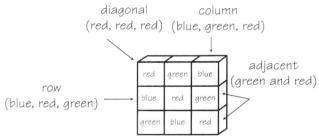

On Their Own

Play *Mystery Grids!*

Here are the rules:

1. This is a game for 2 players. The object is to guess the secret arrangement of 9 Snap Cubes by asking as few questions as possible.

2. Players decide who will be the Grid Maker and who will be the Grid Guesser.

3. The Grid Maker builds a Mystery Grid by:

   ♦ arranging the cubes in a 3-by-3 square.

   ♦ using 3 different colors with 3 cubes in each color.

   ♦ making all cubes of the same color connect along at least 1 face.

 Okay    Not okay

4. When the Grid Maker is ready, the Grid Guesser asks about the color of cubes in a particular row or column.

5. The Grid Maker tells how many cubes of each color are in the row or column, but not the order of the cubes.

6. Players keep track of the number of questions asked.

7. Play until the Grid Maker is ready to have the Mystery Grid revealed.

• Play several games of *Mystery Grid*. Switch roles each time.

• Be ready to talk about good questions and bad questions.

The Bigger Picture

Thinking and Sharing

Invite children to talk about their games and describe some of the thinking they did.

Use prompts like these to promote class discussion:

♦ What did you think about as you planned your questions?

♦ How did you keep track of the answers?

♦ Did you ask any questions that you wanted to take back? Explain.

♦ What questions were particularly good to ask? Why?

Extending the Activity

1. Have children play the game again, but this time use 16 Snap Cubes, four each in four different colors.

2. Have children play the game again, but this time eliminate the rule that same color cubes must be connected along at least one face.

Where's the Mathematics?

An issue that arises as soon as children begin to ask and answer questions about their Mystery Grids is an agreed-upon identification system for the squares in the grids. Children need to clarify what is the top, bottom, left, and right of an arrangement. Some children find that making a 3-by-3 template with labeled squares, as shown, makes communication easier.

C1	C2	C3
C4	C5	C6
C7	C8	C9

Others use an ordered pair system in which the first number indicates the row and the second indicates the column:

(1,1)	(1,2)	(1,3)
(2,1)	(2,2)	(2,3)
(3,1)	(3,2)	(3,3)

There are only two possible basic configurations of the grid. Any other arrangement is merely a flip or rotation of one of these two configurations. The numbers represent the three colors.

Configuration 1

1	1	1
2	2	2
3	3	3

Configuration 2

1	1	2
1	2	2
3	3	3

Children may notice patterns within the configurations as they become more familiar with the game. One such pattern is that at least one row or column has all its cubes the same color (i.e. all three rows in Configuration 1, the third row in Configuration 2). Another pattern is that at least one row or column contains each of the three colors (all three columns in Configuration 1, the second column in Configuration 2).

Guessing the arrangements, or Mystery Grids, fosters logical thinking and deductive reasoning. Children most often use elimination, or guess and check, or a combination of both. At first, children ask more questions than necessary, such as "What's in the first row?" followed by "What's in the first column?" As they become more experienced, children can realize that no matter which row (or column) is asked about first, there are only two possible answers: three of one color or two of one color and one of another color.

If the answer to "What's in the first row?" is "three of one color," a good next question is "What's in an adjacent row?" For example, suppose children are using red, blue, and green cubes. If the answer to "What's in row 1?" is "three reds," the Grid Guesser would be wise to build a train of three red cubes and then ask "What's in row 2?" Two possibilities exist and the solution can be found without having to ask a third question.

(or a flip of this)

If the answer to "What's in the first row?" is "two of one color and one of another color" then four new choices (and their flips) exist. They are shown below along with possible placements for the red cube in the second row.

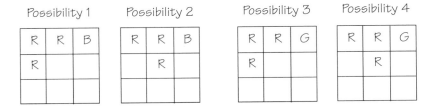

Now a good second question would be "What is in the second row?"

As children consider the different row arrangements, they should be able to conclude R B R (Color 1, Color 2, Color 1) is impossible for any row. Such an arrangement violate the rule that all cubes of the same color must be connected along at least one face.

Some children might, as a strategy, set up the following trains.

For the third cube, children then reason that if the first row is R R R, the result must combine R R, two of the reds in the first row, with R B (or R G) in one of these ways:

Flips of the same arrangement

Asking about the cubes in the diagonal is another strategy for solving the problem. For example, if both diagonals have three different colors, then the Mystery Gird is Configuration 1 or a flip or rotation of Configuration 1.

PAINTED CUBES

PATTERNS/FUNCTIONS • GEOMETRY

- Surface area
- Algebra
- Volume
- Organizing data

Getting Ready

What You'll Need

Snap Cubes, about 150 per group
Stick-on dots (optional)

Overview

Children imagine that cube structures made of Snap Cubes are dipped in paint. They predict how many faces of each Snap Cube would be painted. In this activity, children have the opportunity to:

- ◆ investigate the relationship between volume and surface area of a cube
- ◆ analyze number patterns
- ◆ collect and organize data
- ◆ make predictions and test conjectures

The Activity

Help children visualize the painted and unpainted parts of the two-cube structure by applying stick-on dots to the painted faces of each cube. Then, when you separate the cubes, it will be obvious which faces are not painted.

Introducing

- ◆ Ask children to imagine that you have dipped one white Snap Cube into a special, quick-drying red paint. Explain that all six faces would be red.

- ◆ Then show children two white cubes snapped together. Ask children to describe which faces of the cubes would be red if the two-cube structure were dipped in the red paint. Take apart the structure to point out that only five faces of each cube would be red.

46 *the Super Source™* ◆ Snap™ Cubes ◆ Grades 5-6   ©1996 Cuisenaire Company of America, Inc.

On Their Own

How many faces of each Snap Cube get painted when a cube structure is dipped in paint?

- Work with a group. Imagine that you have to dip larger and larger cube structures into quick-drying paint.

- Use Snap Cubes to build each cube structure starting with a 2 x 2 x 2 cube.

- For each structure, figure out how many Snap Cubes would have 3 faces painted, 2 faces painted, 1 face painted, and 0 faces painted.

- When you build your cube structures, you may want to use 1 color for Snap Cubes with 1 face painted, another color for the Snap Cubes with 2 faces painted, and so on.

- Record your findings and look for patterns.

- Continue investigating until you can figure out how to find the numbers of Snap Cubes with 0, 1, 2, or 3 faces painted in a cube structure of any size.

The Bigger Picture

Thinking and Sharing

Ask children how they organized their data and what number patterns they found. Then, create a class chart with the headings *Dimensions of Cube, # of Snap Cubes, 3 faces painted, 2 faces painted, 1 face painted,* and *0 faces painted.*

Use prompts like these to promote class discussion:

- How did you organize your data?

- What patterns did you find?

- How do these number patterns relate to what is happening with each cube structure?

- Could the number 708 appear in the column labeled *2 faces*? Why or why not?

- Could the number 1,000 appear in the column labeled *1 face?* Why or why not?

- What predictions could you make about a cube structure that has 12 cubes on each edge? How did you arrive at these predictions?

Extending the Activity

Have children repeat the activity for single-layer prisms, starting with a a 1 x 1 x 2 rectangular prism made from two Snap Cubes. They should increase the size of the prism by one unit in length and one in width for each term, that is, 1 x 2 x 3, 1 x 3 x 4, 1 x 4 x 5, and so on.

Where's the Mathematics?

Children's records of the data may look like this:

Dimensions of Cube	# of Snap Cubes	# of Cubes Painted			
		3 faces	2 faces	1 face	0 faces
2 x 2 x 2	8	8	0	0	0
3 x 3 x 3	27	8	12	6	1
4 x 4 x 4	64	8	24	24	8
5 x 5 x 5	125	8	36	54	27
6 x 6 x 6	216	8	48	96	64

As the class analyzes the data, be sure they can see the connections between the numbers on the chart and the actual physical models. It may be helpful to have color-coded models at the front of the class to use during discussion. The Snap Cubes with 1 face painted would be one color, those with 2 faces painted would be another color, and so on.

Looking at their structures and the data in their charts, children are likely to point out that the number of Snap Cubes needed for each cube structure is the product of the dimensions of the cube structure. Although this is not the focus of the activity, this information helps children to check their work since the sum of the painted and unpainted Snap Cubes must equal the total number of cubes in the structure. Some children may point out that this total number of cubes also represents the volume of the structure.

Children will notice that there are always 8 Snap Cubes with three painted faces. These are the Snap Cubes at the vertices of the cube structure. Children can easily verify that every cube, no matter how large, has only 8 vertices.

The Snap Cubes that get paint on two faces are the ones that are along the edges and between the vertices. In a 3 x 3 x 3 cube, there is one such Snap Cube along each of the 12 edges of the cube structure, and so there are 12 cubes with two faces painted. Likewise, in a 4 x 4 x 4 cube structure, there are two such Snap Cubes along each of the 12 edges of the cube structure, and so there are 24 cubes with two faces painted. Since every cube, no matter how large, has 12 edges, the cubes with two faces painted will always be multiples of 12. To find the specific number for a given cube structure, subtract 2 vertex cubes from the number of cubes along the edge of the structure and then multiply that answer by 12. Once children discover this pattern, they should be able to conclude that is possible to have 708 in the *2 faces* column because 708 is a multiple of 12.

The Snap Cubes that have 1 face painted are those that are on the faces of the structure but are not at the vertices nor along the edges. Children will probably recognize that the numbers of Snap Cubes with 1 face painted are multiples of 6 because every cube, no matter how large, has exactly six faces. Since 1,000 is not a multiple of 6, children should be able to conclude that there is no cube structure with 1,000 in the column labeled *1 face*. If children have color-coded their structures, they will notice that the Snap Cubes with 1 face painted form a square with dimensions 2 less than the face of the cube.

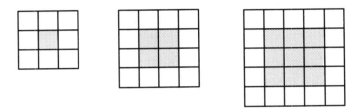

Children may be able to come up with a generalization for finding the number of Snap Cubes with one face painted: *Subtract 2 from the dimension of the cube and square that answer. Then you multiply by 6 because there are 6 faces on a cube.*

The Snap Cubes in the structure that don't need any paint will be "hidden" in the center. The number of Snap Cubes with 0 painted faces is always the number of Snap Cubes in the cube structure that has dimensions 2 less than the one being described. For example, a 4 x 4 x 4 cubes has 64 Snap Cubes. Inside, there is a 2 x 2 x 2 cube that no one can see. And so, 2 x 2 x 2 or 8 Snap Cubes have no painted faces.

This activity provides children with practice in visualizing and finding patterns and lays the foundation for future work with algebraic functions and variables.

PENTACUBES I

- Spatial visualization
- Congruence
- Transformational geometry

Getting Ready

What You'll Need

Snap Cubes, 10 of 1 color
per pair

Snap Cube grid paper, page 91

Isometric dot paper (optional)

Overhead Snap Cubes and Isometric
dot paper transparency (optional)

Overview

Children search for different ways to arrange five Snap Cubes so that each
arrangement, or pentacube, lies flat on a desktop. In this activity, children
have the opportunity to:

- ◆ create and compare three-dimensional figures with the same volume
- ◆ verify that three-dimensional figures are non-congruent
- ◆ discover that figures with the same volume may not look alike

The Activity

*Use Snap Cubes of the same color so
children concentrate on the figure, not
the color, when deciding whether two
figures are the same or not.*

*If they are familiar with isometric dot
paper, children can record on it as
well as on grid paper.*

Introducing

- ◆ Ask children to use their cubes to determine if it is possible to
arrange three Snap Cubes in more than one way.
- ◆ Have volunteers describe and display their
arrangements.
- ◆ Establish that only two figures are possible.
- ◆ Show children how to determine that
these figures are the same by rotating or
flipping the figures until one fits exactly
over the other.
- ◆ Model how to record the top view of these figures on grid paper.

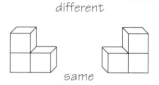

different

same

On Their Own

How many different pentacubes that lie flat can you make with 5 Snap Cubes?

- Work with a partner. Each of you make a figure with 5 Snap Cubes. Such a figure is called a *pentacube*. Be sure that when you put your pentacube down, it can be turned so that every cube touches your desktop at once.

Okay   Not Okay

- Compare your pentacubes.
    - If they are different, record the top view of both on Snap Cube grid paper.
    - If they are the same, record the top view of only 1 figure.
- Try to build another pentacube that is different from what you just built.
- Continue building pentacubes until you can't make any more that are different from what you already have.
- Be ready to explain why you think you have found all the flat pentacubes.

The Bigger Picture

Thinking and Sharing

Have volunteers take turns reconstructing a Snap Cube figure, each time checking with the class that it is different from those already shown. Continue until the class agrees that all the different flat pentacubes are on display.

Use prompts such as these to promote class discussion:

- How many different figures did you find?
- How are these two pentacubes different from each other?
- How do you know that you have found all of the possible flat pentacubes?

Drawing and Writing

Have children use pictures and words to prove that there are 12 non-congruent flat pentacubes.

Extending the Activity

1. Have children predict which of the grid paper shapes can be folded to form an open-top box. For each prediction, tell children to mark the bottom of the box with an "X." Then direct them to cut out and fold their shapes to check their predictions.

Teacher Talk

Where's the Mathematics?

This activity helps children discover that figures with the same volume do not always look alike. It also focuses on congruence. As they build and compare their pentacubes, children flip or rotate their figures either mentally or physically to make sure they are indeed different.

In this activity, children have the opportunity to hear and use geometric terms. The number of cubes used in a three-dimensional figure is its volume. The flat sides of the figure are called its faces. The edges refer to the line segments where the faces meet. A corner of the figure is called the vertex. Each Snap Cube has a volume of one, six square faces, twelve edges, and eight vertices. Each pentacube has a volume of five, but the numbers of faces, edges, and vertices vary.

Twelve flat pentacubes are possible.

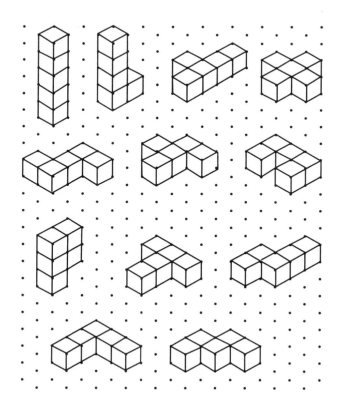

2. Have children cut out their grid paper shapes and arrange them in a straight line so that each succeeding shape may be made from the preceding shape by moving only one Snap Cube.

3. Have children find the surface area of each pentacube and describe what they notice.

Initially, many children approach the task in a very random manner. When they begin to explore whether they have exhausted all the possibilities, they may try to develop a system. For example, they may start with five cubes in a row and then move one cube to find all the possible figures that could be made with only four cubes in a single row. Then they may explore all the figures possible with only three cubes in the row. Other children may make one of the figures and then move only cube to find the next shape and then move only one cube in that shape to find the next one and so forth.

Mathematicians call the two-dimensional representations of the figures that the children made on grid paper *pentominoes*. *Penta* is the Greek root for five and *ominoes* refers to the square shapes that make up the whole figure. Because the shapes can be rotated to look like certain letters of the alphabet, children often come up with the following labeling system to identify each figure.

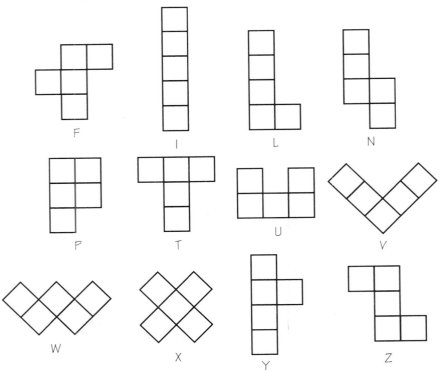

You may wish to continue further explorations with pentacubes in the lessons entitled "Pentacubes II" and "Penta Nets."

PENTACUBES II

- Spatial visualization
- Congruence
- Transformational geometry

Getting Ready

What You'll Need

Snap Cubes, 100 per group

Isometric dot paper, page 90 (optional)

Overview

Children search for different ways to arrange five Snap Cubes so that each arrangement, no matter how it is placed on a table, has at least one cube that does not touch the table. In this activity, children have the opportunity to:

- ◆ develop their spatial sense
- ◆ see how reflection affects solid geometric figures

The Activity

This lesson is an extension of Pentacubes I *(page 50)*. However, the outcome of this lesson does not depend on the outcomes of Pentacubes I, and could easily be done independently of that lesson.

Use Snap Cubes of the same color so children concentrate on the figure, not the color, when deciding whether two figures are the same or not.

Introducing

- ◆ Ask children to use their Snap Cubes to determine if it is possible to make a figure in which all four Snap Cubes do not touch the tabletop.

- ◆ Have volunteers hold up their different arrangements and talk about them. Three figures are possible.

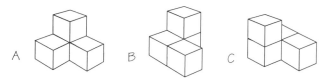

- ◆ Some children may initially think that figures B and C are the same. Show them that no matter how you try to rotate or flip these two figures, you cannot get C to look exactly like B.

On Their Own

How many different figures can you make with 5 Snap Cubes so that at least 1 of the 5 cubes does not touch the tabletop?

- Work with a group. Each of you makes a figure with 5 cubes. Make the figures so that no matter how you place them on a table at least 1 cube does *not* touch the table.

Okay  Not okay

- Compare your figures.
  - ◆ If they are all different, keep them all.
  - ◆ If some of them are the same, keep only 1 of each different figure.
- Continue to build and compare figures, keeping only those figures that are different from what you have already built.
- Continue building figures until you can't make any more that are different from what you already have.

The Bigger Picture

Thinking and Sharing

Have volunteers, one at a time, display a figure they found. Call on children to bring up any figures that match the ones on display and group like figures together. Continue until all the different figures found are on display.

Use prompts such as these to promote class discussion:

- ◆ What was easy about making the figures? What was hard?
- ◆ How are these two figures different from each other?
- ◆ What do you notice about these two figures? (Hold up two figures that are mirror images.)
- ◆ Did you find any other pairs that were mirror images of each other?
- ◆ Did you have a strategy for finding the different figures? If so, what was it?
- ◆ How many figures did you find? Do you think you found them all? Why do you think so?

Writing

Have children choose two of the pentacube figures and describe how the two shapes are alike and how they are different.

Extending the Activity

1. If children are familiar with isometric dot paper, have them record their figures on it.

Where's the Mathematics?

Children have an easy time building a variety of pentacube figures. The challenge arises in determining whether the shape is unique or not. Many children will need to handle the models physically, turning, flipping, and rotating them before they are convinced of their uniqueness or of their congruency to a shape already made. Studying the models this closely will provide valuable background for later, more formal studies in solid geometry.

The nineteen possible shapes are shown here. Do not expect that all groups will discover all of them.

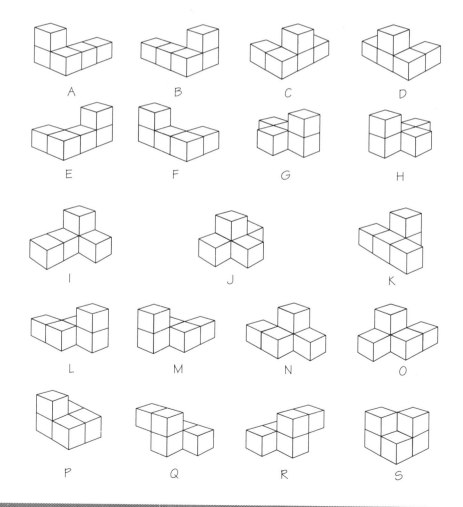

2. Ask children to select one of the pentacube figures and draw it on isometric dot paper. Have them return the pentacube figure to a pile of figures made by several other children. Then have children exchange isometric drawings to see if they can match the drawings with the actual figures.

Of the nineteen shapes, there are seven pairs of mirror images: A and B, C and D, E and F, G and H, L and M, N and O, and Q and R. No matter how these pairs are turned, flipped, or rotated, it will be impossible to make the two shapes look identical. They will look like the reflection one would see in a mirror.

Initially, many children will approach the task of finding all possible figures in a very random manner. When they begin to wonder whether they have exhausted all the possibilities, they may try to develop a "system". For example, they may start with four cubes arranged as an "L" on the tabletop and then move the fifth cube to find all of its possible locations that will create a new figure that satisfies the condition that all five cubes may not touch the tabletop. Then they may explore all the figures possible with only three cubes in the row and finally with only two in a row. Other children may make one of the figures and then move only cube to find the next shape and then move only one cube in that shape to find the next one and so forth. For children who have discovered the mirror property that many of the figures possess, they may make a figure and then see if it has a unique mirror partner to go with it.

PENTA NETS

- Spatial visualization
- Surface area

Getting Ready

What You'll Need

Snap Cubes, 3 per child

Snap Cube grid paper, 1/2 sheet per child, page 91

Scissors, 1 pair per child

Tape

Empty cereal or cookie box that has been opened up and laid flat

Overview

Children build a structure with three Snap Cubes and draw a grid paper net that could be used to cover the structure. In this activity, children have the opportunity to:

- ◆ increase their spatial visualization skills
- ◆ work with surface area in a non-computational way
- ◆ work with two-dimensional and three-dimensional geometry

The Activity

Tell children to ignore the Snap Cube's connector post when they make their nets.

Introducing

- ◆ Show children the flattened box and tell them that designers have to think about what packages will look like when they are cut out of cardboard before they are folded up. These flattened shapes are called *nets*.

- ◆ Ask children to make a net on grid paper for one Snap Cube.

- ◆ Invite a few volunteers to come to the chalkboard and share their nets. Have them place the Snap Cube against one of the squares on the board and describe how the net will be wrapped around the cube after the net is cut out.

- ◆ Have children cut out their nets and fold them to see if they make the cube.

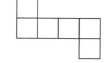

On Their Own

Can you design nets that could be used to make a Snap Cube structure?

- Work with a partner. Each partner uses 3 Snap Cubes to build this structure.

- Each partner designs and records a net that could be used to build a replica of this structure.

    A *net* is a pattern that folds to make a 3-dimensional figure. Here are 3 different examples of nets, each of which folds to form a single cube.

    Nets for a cube

    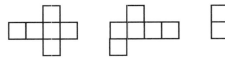

- Show your design to your partner and discuss whether it looks as if it will work. Make any changes in the design.

- When you are convinced that the 2 nets work, transfer your sketches to grid paper.

- Cut the nets out and fold them to see if they work. If a net doesn't work, revise the design until it does.

- Make a clean copy of your nets (unfolded) to share with the class.

The Bigger Picture

Thinking and Sharing

Invite children to show their nets. Have children sort them into categories of roughly the same design.

Use prompts such as these to promote class discussion:

- How many squares of grid paper were required to make a net?

- Can you find two (or more) nets that are almost identical? How are they the same? How are they different?

- Which net(s) require the smallest rectangle of graph paper? What are the dimensions of that rectangle?

- What percent of the rectangle was used to make the shape? What percent was not used?

- What was the hardest part of designing the net?

- Did you have to design more than one net before you got a design that worked? How did you improve the first design to make it work?

Drawing and Writing

Have children write a step-by-step explanation of how their net can be folded to form the structure. Ask them to illustrate their steps with drawings.

Where's the Mathematics?

Translating a three-dimensional shape into a two-dimensional net requires a great deal of spatial visualization. Many children need to make more than one net before they are successful. Often their nets have only one or two misplaced squares. Once they have folded the net, however, they see where the problem lies and how to correct it. A frequent method of correction is to snip off the offending squares and use tape to affix them to the net in the correct position. Encourage children who have used the tape approach to redraw the net properly to show to the class. Making a sketch on plain paper and discussing that sketch with their partner before they transfer to it to grid paper will allow greater opportunity for children to analyze how they are approaching the problem. Working directly on graph paper leads to a more trial-and-error approach.

The surface area of the structure in this activity is 14 square units, so 14 squares of grid paper will be required to build the structure. If children check to make sure their net covers 14 squares before they cut it out, many errors will be avoided. Many children have difficulty because they hold the shape in one hand while trying to record their sketch of a net. They move the shape and get confused about what they have done and what remains to be done. One way they can avoid this confusion is to place the shape directly on the paper, trace around it and then, leaving it in place, imagine how they have to add squares in order to be able to wrap the shape completely in paper.

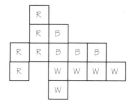

Some children will find that color coding the drawing helps them keep track of where they have already been. For example, if a child had a shape that used a black, a red, and a white Snap Cube, the drawing might look like this:

The squares marked B indicate that those squares will be used to cover the black Snap Cube; W will cover the white cube, and R will cover the red

Extending the Activity

1. Have children cut out four copies of the net they designed. Ask them to show how to arrange those copies on one sheet of grid paper to minimize the leftover paper.

2. Ask children to repeat the activity using four Snap Cubes. You may assign the shape or let them choose one of their own design.

---

cube. This method breaks the problem into smaller solutions that can be combined to solve the big problem. It also allows children to identify how the net was first oriented before it was cut out and folded.

The hardest thing for most children is imagining the squares that need to be added so that the top of the figure will be covered. Many can draw the bottom and side squares making the net an open-top box, but after that, they are unsure where to add the squares needed to cover the top. Physically lifting the paper around the shape and asking children "Where is the paper that is going to go over the top of the shape in relation to the squares that you have already drawn?" helps some children see that the squares for the top are added to the squares used for the sides.

When they compare their nets, children may be surprised that there are so many solutions. Some of the nets will vary only by one or two squares, such as this example where the square marked with an "x" has been moved but everything else has remained the same. In the right hand sketch the lines on the top and left of the square marked with an "x" must be cut so this square may be folded up.

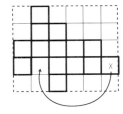 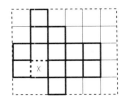

The net shown on the left above requires a rectangle of grid paper that measures 6 by 5 squares while the net on the right requires a 5-by-5 rectangle. The net on the left uses 14 out of 30 squares, or about 47% of the paper and wastes 16 squares or 53%. The right-hand net uses 14 out of 25 squares, or 56% of the paper, wasting 44% of the paper. The right-hand net would be a more "efficient" use of resources. Children could be challenged in Extension #1 to make another interesting comparison of efficiencies.

For many children, this will be their first experience linking plane and solid geometry. Seeing the application of these ideas in the concept of packaging helps children see the relevance of what they study in school.

POINT OF VIEW

Getting Ready

What You'll Need

Snap Cubes, 15–30 per child

Snap Cube grid paper, 1 sheet per child, page 91

Paper lunch bag, 1 per child

Books or heavy folders to serve as barriers (optional)

Adhesive dots (optional)

Overhead Snap Cubes and/or Snap Cube grid paper transparency (optional)

Overview

Children build structures with Snap Cubes and draw them from six different views. Then they reverse the process by building structures from the views. In this activity, children have the opportunity to:

◆ draw a three-dimensional figure in two dimensions

◆ learn about the advantages and limitations of a two-dimensional representation of a three-dimensional shape

◆ visualize the relationships between the views, both three-dimensionally and two-dimensionally

The Activity

Adhesive dot to indicate front.

Introducing

◆ Build a three-story Snap Cube structure like the one shown at the left. Mark the front with an adhesive dot or piece of tape.

◆ Ask children how many ways they can view the structure. Identify the six points of view of your structure: front, right side, back, left side, top, and bottom.

◆ Draw the front, top, and right side of your structure on a grid and have children compare these to the structure.

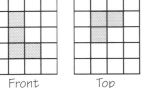

Front   Top   Right side

◆ Point out that each time you draw a view, you start with the front of the structure facing you.

On Their Own

From point-of-view drawings, can you build a Snap Cube structure that exactly matches another?

- Work with a partner. Each of you should build a structure you like with 10 to 15 cubes. Make your structure at least 2 stories high. Keep your structures hidden from each other.

- Draw all six views on grid paper and label them—*front, back, right side, left side, top,* and *bottom*. Here are the six views for a simple 5-cube structure.

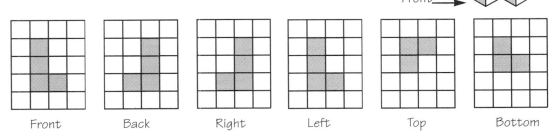

Front →

| Front | Back | Right | Left | Top | Bottom |

- Hide your structure in a paper bag.

- Exchange point-of-view drawings with your partner. Use the drawings to build your partner's structure.

- Compare the structure you built with the structure in the bag.

- Discuss what happened with your partner.

The Bigger Picture

Thinking and Sharing

Have the volunteers share their structures and drawings and describe what they noticed.

Use prompts like these to promote class discussion:

- ◆ Which did you like better: drawing the views of the structure or building the structure from the views? Why?

- ◆ What was hard about drawing the views? easy?

- ◆ What was hard about building a structure from the point-of-view drawings? easy?

- ◆ What strategies did you use when building from the views?

- ◆ Did your structure match your partner's views but not the structure? Why?

- ◆ How are the six views of your structure the same? How are they different?

- ◆ Is it possible to make a structure that looks the same from all six views? Explain.

Extending the Activity

1. Have children repeat the activity with this change: Use only the top, right side, and bottom views.

2. Introduce the concept of floor mat, a rectangular bottom view that tells how many cubes are in each column of the structure. Then have children repeat the activity, but this time, have them also make a floor mat.

Teacher Talk

Where's the Mathematics?

There are a number of approaches children might use in building the structures from the drawings. Some may start by looking at the bottom view and build a structure that is one cube high, and then look at the front view and add cubes to make towers as tall as indicated in the front view. Finally, they will look at the side views and remove any extra cubes. This method will yield a structure with the greatest possible number of cubes.

Other children may use a trial-and-error approach of randomly adding or removing cubes until the structure matches all the drawings. They will build from the views in no particular order and alter the structure as needed with each added view. This approach requires constant checking and rechecking to ensure that views are all accurate and are based on all the information given.

No matter what approach children use, they should recognize the importance of being accurate and of checking that all information has been correctly used.

As children draw the views of their structures they may discover that the top and bottom, the front and back, and the right and left sides are either mirror images of one another or exactly the same. For example, in this 11-cube structure, the right and left side views are identical, the front and back views are mirror images with a vertical line of reflection, and the top and bottom views are mirror images with a horizontal line of reflection.

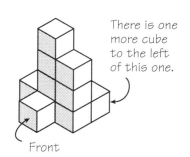

There is one more cube to the left of this one.

Front

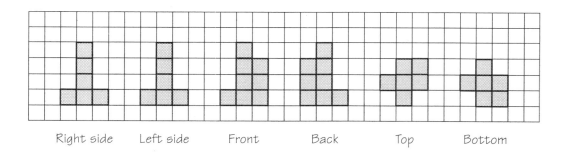

Right side   Left side   Front   Back   Top   Bottom

3. If children have had experience using isometric dot paper, have them repeat the activity with this addition: Make dot paper drawings of the structures. Collect the drawings and create task cards. On one side of the card show the grid paper views; on the other side, show an isometric drawing of one solution. Use the cards throughout the school year and have children provide drawings of other solutions.

Children may also notice that having all the views does not ensure a structure that will be exactly the same as the original. For example, these two different structures have the same six views.

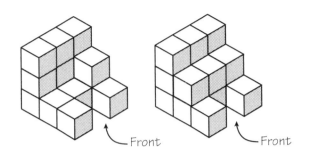

In cases such as the one above, children will realize that more information is needed for duplicating a structure. This might be an opportune time to bring up the concept of a floor mat, a rectangular grid that tells how many cubes are in each column. Children might like to think of a floor mat as a "bird's eye view" of a structure. The structure in the *Introducing* section has this floor mat:

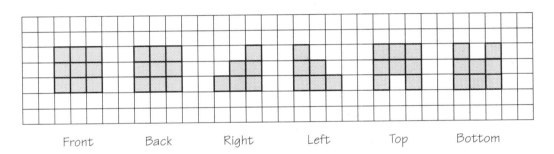

Front   Back   Right   Left   Top   Bottom

3	1
1	0

This activity should be revisited throughout the school year since it engages children in skills that have real-life applications. To be successful at understanding operating directions for appliances or interpreting diagrams that explain how to assemble a bicycle or a toy or a piece of furniture requires moving confidently between two-dimensional and three-dimensional thinking.

PUTTING IT ALL TOGETHER

- Spatial visualization
- Following directions
- Deductive reasoning

Getting Ready

What You'll Need

Snap Cubes, 15 per pair
Isometric dot paper, page 90 (optional)
Paper bags for saving structures

Overview

Children build Snap Cube structures and then write clues that allow other children to build the same structure in the same colors. In this activity, children have the opportunity to:

- ◆ develop spatial visualization and logical reasoning skills
- ◆ use geometric language in a context
- ◆ write with precision and clarity

The Activity

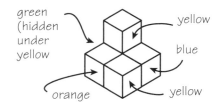

green (hidden under yellow   yellow

blue

orange   yellow

Introducing

- ◆ Build the Snap Cube structure shown at the left but keep it hidden.
- ◆ Invite children to solve the following riddle. Give one clue at a time. Each time you give a clue, tell children to show it with the cubes.

  Clue 1: My structure has five Snap Cubes. One of them is green.
  Clue 2: Two of my Snap Cubes are the same color.
  Clue 3: A yellow cube is next to the orange cube.
  Clue 4: The faces of the orange cube and the blue cube do not touch.
  Clue 5: The blue cube and three other cubes form a square.
  Clue 6: The yellow cubes touch at only one corner.

- ◆ After the final clue, show your structure. Have children compare and discuss their results.

On Their Own

Can you create and solve Snap Cube riddles?

- Work with a partner. Build a Snap Cube structure using at least 6, but no more than 15, Snap Cubes.

- Create a riddle that describes your structure.

- Write at least 4, but no more than 8, clues for your riddle.

- Hide the structure in a paper bag. Then close the bag and clip your riddle to the bag.

- Exchange your riddle with another pair of partners. Solve one another's riddles.

- Compare your results and discuss the thinking you did.

The Bigger Picture

Thinking and Sharing

Have volunteers share the structure they made and what happened as they solved each other's riddles.

Use prompts such as these to promote class discussion:

- Which did you find easier: writing clues or following clues? Explain.

- What happened as you tried to solve someone else's riddle? Which words or clues were not clear enough? Which words were the most helpful?

- Did any riddles have more than one solution? If so, how could you change the clues so that there is only one solution?

- What tips would you give someone about creating a structure? about writing riddles?

Collect the riddles and use them to create a set of task cards that can be used throughout the school year.

Writing

Have children explain which they prefer: writing riddles or solving riddles.

Extending the Activity

1. Have children write a riddle with more than one solution. Then ask them to add appropriate clues to give the riddle only one solution.

2. Have children write a riddle that contains clues with conflicting information so there is no solution. Then have them rewrite the riddle so that there is only one solution.

Where's the Mathematics?

This activity reveals to children how difficult it can be to accurately describe an object using only words. It also helps them see how differently two people can interpret the same words.

When children solve the riddles, they are using deductive reasoning, a process in which they use given information to arrive at a conclusion. They use the Snap Cubes to model the information given in the hypothesis (the clues) and arrive at a unique conclusion (the structure). When they create their own riddles, they are working backwards in the sense that they start with the conclusion (the structure) and determine the hypothesis (the clues) that lead to the structure. Children who are primarily visual learners may say that they prefer to create rather than solve riddles because they like to start with the final structure in their mind. Children who are primarily tactile learners may prefer to solve riddles because they like to manipulate the cube shapes. Whether children are creating or solving riddles, it is more important to focus on how children weigh information rather than on who gets a "correct" solution. The correct solutions will come as children become adept at interpreting information.

The order in which children look at the clues is not important. Some children may prefer to look at all the clues at once and start with the clue that is easiest for them to follow. For example, in the riddle in the Introducing section, children who are primarily tactile learners may feel more comfortable starting with Clue 3 because it focuses on the placement of the cubes rather than on the number or the color of the cubes.

As children create and then solve riddles throughout the school year, they can gain an appreciation for using precise mathematical language. For example, in each of the three cases below, a child might simply describe the purple and green cubes as touching. Yet, saying that a face of the purple covers a face of the green (first figure), or that an edge of the purple runs along the edge of the green (second figure), or that a corner of the purple touches a corner of the green (third figure) is so much more explicit and helpful.

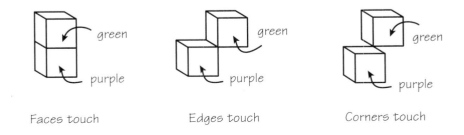

Faces touch   Edges touch   Corners touch

With practice, children learn to provide additional information or establish a common understanding to clarify terms such as *above*, *left*, *below*, *next to*, *between*, and *adjacent* that may be open to interpretation.

If children have had experience using isometric dot paper or can draw in perspective, encourage them to use drawings to record their structures. These drawings can be placed in the bags instead of the structures. Some children will take advantage of the opportunity to record their structures with drawings. However, producing a three-dimensional figure in two dimensions is a demanding task for children at this level. If they appear to be getting frustrated, encourage them to persevere and emphasize that this kind of skill will come with continued practice.

PYRAMID NUMBERS

- Pyramid numbers
- Pattern recognition
- Growth patterns

Getting Ready

What You'll Need

Snap Cubes, 80–90 per pair

Calculators, 1 per pair

Snap Cube grid paper, page 91, (optional)

Crayons (optional)

Overhead Snap Cubes and/or Snap Cube grid paper transparency (optional)

Overview

Using Snap Cubes, children build models of pyramid numbers. They record data about each structure, look for patterns, and make conjectures. In this activity, children have the opportunity to:

- ◆ represent a numerical sequence geometrically
- ◆ collect and analyze data
- ◆ learn about a predictable growth pattern
- ◆ use patterns to make predictions

The Activity

Introducing

- ◆ Display one Snap Cube. Then cover the top and all the sides of the cube with cubes of a different color.

- ◆ Display the new structure. Ask children to predict how many cubes will be needed to cover the top and all the sides of every exposed Snap Cube in the structure. Then, using cubes of a third color, make your structure look like the one shown at the right.

- ◆ Count the cubes to confirm that 13 were needed.

- ◆ Explain that since the Snap Cube structures you made look like pyramids, the number of cubes they contain—1, 6, and 19—are called *pyramid numbers*.

On Their Own

Is there a way to know in advance the number of Snap Cubes you would need and how to connect them in order to build a pyramid of any size?

- Work with a partner to build pyramids that look like these:

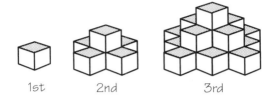

- Keep track of the number of cubes you add each time, the total number of cubes in each pyramid, and the patterns you find.

- Predict what the 4th pyramid will look like, then build it.

- Build pyramids until you can use your findings to describe, in detail, the 10th pyramid without building it.

The Bigger Picture

Thinking and Sharing

Create a class chart with three columns. Label the first column *Pyramid Number*, the second column *Number of Cubes Added*, and the third column *Total Number of Cubes*. Have children fill in the chart and discuss the data.

Use prompts such as these to promote class discussion:

- What did you notice as you built bigger and bigger pyramids?

- What patterns do you notice in the data?

- How many structures did you need to build before you could make predictions about the tenth pyramid? Why?

- How did you find the number of cubes needed for the tenth pyramid?

- How is the tenth pyramid different from the ninth pyramid? from the eleventh pyramid?

If children have done "Triangular Number Sequence," "Squares and Staircases," and "Greek Cross Numbers," have them take out their work from those activities to compare to findings in this activity.

Writing

Ask children to describe the fifteenth pyramid number and explain their thinking.

Extending the Activity

Have children repeat this activity, but make the structures grow in six directions.

Where's the Mathematics?

The first ten pyramid numbers are the numbers that appear in the third column of the class chart, shown below. The second column contains a set of numbers known as Greek Cross numbers, the first column contains the set of counting numbers. All three number sequences grow in predictable ways.

Pyramid Number	Number of Cubes Added	Total Number of Cubes
1	0	1
2	5	6
3	13	19
4	25	44
5	41	85
6	61	146
7	85	231
8	113	344
9	145	489
10	181	670

Since they purposely are not given enough Snap Cubes to build every pyramid, this activity provides children with the opportunity to do mental and calculator computation, pattern searching, and conjecturing.

After building three or four pyramids, children start to notice patterns. They may see the symmetry of their pyramids and think of each pyramid as four staircases all converging on the same top step. Thus, to get the next pyramid means covering each stair step, adding one to the top, and filling in the corners.

Some children look at each pyramid as a set of horizontal layers and notice that the number of layers is the same as the pyramid number. For example, pyramid 2 has two layers, a one-cube layer and a five-cube layer. Pyramid 3 has three layers with 1, 5, and 13 cubes in each layer, respectively.

Children who look at the growing pyramid from a bird's eye view will notice that each layer adds multiples of four to the previous one. In any pyramid, the second layer from the top can be looked at as 1 + 4, the third layer as 1 + 4 + 8, and the fourth as 1 + 4 + 8 + 12. The sums of each of these series produces the Greek Cross number sequence 1, 5, 13, 25, ...

Still focusing on the physical structures, children can notice that the bottom layer shows rows of consecutive odd numbers of cubes. The pyramid number dictates how long the series is before it repeats. For example, the bottom layer of pyramid 2 involves the two odd numbers, 1 and 3, and can be thought of as 1 + 3 + 1. Pyramid 3 involves three odd numbers, and could be viewed as is 1 + 3 + 5 + 3 + 1. This same pattern of consecutive odd numbers can be seen if the pyramid is viewed from the side. In this case, the odd numbers represent the number of new cubes added. It follows the same ascending/descending pattern. For the fourth pyramid, 1 + 3 + 5 + 7 + 5 + 3 + 1, or 25, new cubes were added.

Each pyramid can also be thought of as a set of staircases. Pyramid 2 can be separated into 3 staircases, comprised of 1 + 4 + 1 cubes, respectively. Pyramid 3 can be separated into 5 staircases, 1 + 4 + 9 + 4 + 1 cubes, respectively. The number of cubes in the tallest staircase is the pyramid number squared. For example, the tallest staircase in pyramid 3 has 3^2, or 9, cubes.

In addition, the number of staircases is always double the number of the pyramid less 1. Pyramid 3 has (2 x 3) − 1, or 5, staircases; pyramid 4 has (2 x 4) − 1, or 7, staircases.

The number of cubes needed to build the tenth pyramid can be found by looking at its horizontal layers. Specifically, it requires 670 cubes, which is the sum of 1 + 5 + 13 + 25 + 41 + 61 + 85 +113 + 145 + 181, the sum of its ten layers of cubes. In terms of staircases, the total number of cubes in the tenth pyramid can be found by adding successive ascending and descending square numbers: $1^2 + 2^2 + 3^2 + 4^2 + 5^2 + 6^2 + 7^2 + 8^2 + 9^2 + 10^2 + 9^2 + 8^2 + 7^2 + 6^2 + 5^2 + 4^2 + 3^2 + 2^2 + 1^2$, or 670 cubes.

SQUARES AND STAIRCASES

Getting Ready

What You'll Need

Snap Cubes, 50–60 per pair

Calculators, 1 per pair

Snap Cube grid paper, page 91 (optional)

Crayons (optional)

Overhead Snap Cubes and/or Snap Cube grid paper transparency (optional)

Overview

Children use Snap Cubes to build a non-typical model of square numbers. They record data, look for patterns, and make conjectures. In this activity, children have the opportunity to:

◆ represent a numerical sequence geometrically

◆ collect and analyze data

◆ learn about a predictable growth pattern

◆ use patterns to make predictions

The Activity

Use any combination of colors. The different colors help children focus on the change in the number of cubes from one staircase to the next.

Introducing

◆ Display a red Snap Cube. Identify the six faces of the cube: the top, bottom, right, left, front, and back.

◆ Tell children that you would like to build a staircase by adding a white cube to the top, left, and right faces. Ask how many white cubes you will need. Add the white cubes and count to confirm that the new staircase contains four cubes.

◆ Ask children what the staircase would look like if you again added cubes—this time blue ones—to the top, left, and right faces of the four-cube staircase.

◆ Have children share their predictions, then add the blue cubes.

◆ Display the new staircase, which now has a total of nine cubes.

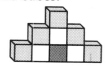

On Their Own

> Is there a way to know in advance the number of Snap Cubes you would need and how to connect them in order to build a staircase of any size?
>
> - Work with a partner to build staircases that look like these:
>
>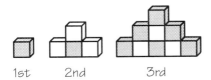
>
> 1st   2nd   3rd
>
> - Keep track of the number of cubes you add each time, the total number of cubes in each staircase, and the patterns you find.
>
> - Predict what the 4th staircase will look like, then build it.
>
> - Build staircases until you can use your findings to describe, in detail, the 100th staircase without building it.

The Bigger Picture

Thinking and Sharing

Create a class chart that has three columns. Label the first column *Staircase Number*, the second column *Number of Cubes Added*, and the third column, *Total Number of Cubes*. Have children fill in the chart and discuss the data.

Use prompts such as these to promote class discussion:

- What did you notice as you built bigger and bigger staircases?

- What patterns do you see in the data?

- How many structures did you need to build before you could make predictions about the 100th staircase?

- How did you find the number of cubes needed for the 100th staircase?

- How is the 100th staircase different from the 99th staircase? from the 101st staircase?

- Mathematicians call the number sequence generated by the total number of cubes *square numbers*. Why do you think they are called square numbers?

Extending the Activity

1. Have children graph their data. On one graph, the numbers along the horizontal axis can represent the "Staircase Number" and the numbers along the vertical axis can represent the "Number of Cubes Added." On a second graph, have children change the vertical axis so it represents the "Total Number of Cubes." Have children compare their graphs.

2. Have children describe, in detail, a staircase whose bottom step contains 41 cubes.

Where's the Mathematics?

This activity provides a fresh approach to looking at square numbers. Generally, the sequence is studied by building larger and larger cubes and focusing on their square faces. Building square numbers in a new fashion helps children to become more open and flexible in their thinking. This activity provides children with an opportunity to use mental math as they analyze the patterns they find.

The class chart should look like this.

Staircase Number	Number of Cubes Added	Total Number of Cubes
1	0	1
2	3	4
3	5	9
4	7	16
5	9	25
6	11	36
7	13	49
8	15	64
9	17	81
10	19	100

Looking at their structures, children can notice many patterns. To begin, every staircase number has a matching number of stairsteps, or layers. That is, staircase 1 has one layer, staircase 2 has two layers, and so on. Every staircase has one cube at the top, and each layer has an odd number of cubes. In addition, all the staircases have symmetry. A vertical line of symmetry goes through the tallest column of cubes in each staircase.

There is more than one way to build a staircase. Some children add one cube to each exposed face on the left, right, and top. Others add a bottom layer that has two more cubes than the bottom layer of the previous staircase. This means that the number of cubes added is always the same as the number of cubes in the bottom layer.

When asked to describe the numbers in the "Total Number of Cubes" column, children usually recognize that each number is the staircase number multiplied by itself. Identify these numbers as *square numbers*. Encourage children to explain why a staircase that looks roughly like a triangle can show square numbers. If no one can provide an explanation, give a hint by splitting a staircase into two pieces, as shown below. Suggest to children that they rotate and move the two pieces to form a square.

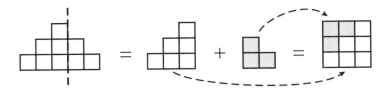

Children will describe the "Number of Cubes Added" column in a variety of ways. The most obvious will be the sequence of odd numbers. Others will describe it as the new "total number of cubes" minus the previous "total number of cubes," that is, $3 = 4 - 1$, $5 = 9 - 4$, $7 = 16 - 9$, and so on. Others may say that it is the staircase number plus the staircase number less one, that is, $3 = 2 + 1$, $5 = 3 + 2$, $7 = 4 + 3$, and so on. These children might point this out on the staircase itself.

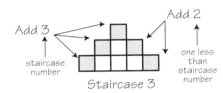

Add 3   Add 2

staircase number

one less than staircase number

Staircase 3

Once they recognize and describe the growth patterns they find in their staircases and their data, children can describe any size staircase. For example, staircase 8 has 8 layers and 64 cubes. This is so since $8 \times 8 = 64$ and $1 + 3 + 5 + 7 + 11 + 13 + 15 = 64$. The 100th staircase is 100 layers high and contains 100×100 or 10,000 cubes. It has 199 more cubes that the 99th staircase.

Encourage children to think in a different way. Tell them how many cubes are in the bottom layer of a staircase, then ask them to predict how many layers, or stairsteps, are in the staircase. To illustrate, imagine a staircase with a base layer of 41 cubes. Some children will work backwards, using the pattern they found to describe the "number of cubes added." For example, if they realize that the "number of cubes added" is twice the staircase number minus one, they may think "If two times a number minus 1 is 41, then two times that number is 42, which means that the number must be 21." Other children may extend their chart until they get to 41. No matter the method, children should find that a staircase with a bottom layer of 41 is the 21st staircase and has a total 21×21 or 441 cubes.

SURFACE AREA WITH 12 CUBES

- Surface area
- Volume

Getting Ready

What You'll Need

Snap Cubes, about 50 per pair
Isometric dot paper, page 90
Stick-on dots (optional)

Overview

Children investigate the range of surface areas possible for different structures made with twelve Snap Cubes. In this activity, children have the opportunity to:

- ◆ discover that surface area can change while volume remains constant

- ◆ notice that different-looking structures with the same volume can have the same surface area

- ◆ generalize that long, thin structures have more surface area than compact, cube-like structures with the same volume

- ◆ find the surface area of a variety of structures

The Activity

Some children may find it helpful to place a stick-on dot on each square face as they count.

Introducing

- ◆ Build this structure.

- ◆ Explain that volume describes the amount of space the structure occupies and is found by counting the number of Snap Cubes.

- ◆ Explain that surface area describes the total area of the outside surface of the structure. It is found by counting the number of the square Snap Cube faces.

- ◆ Ask children to duplicate your structure and find its volume and surface area. Verify that they are 5 and 22, respectively.

- ◆ Show how to record the structure on isometric dot paper. Record its surface area.

On Their Own

> ### What is the smallest possible surface area for a structure built with 12 Snap Cubes? What is the largest possible surface area?
>
> - Work with a partner. Each of you builds a structure with 12 Snap Cubes and finds its surface area.
>
> - Record the structure and its surface area on isometric dot paper.
>
> - Compare your structures. If they have the same surface area, keep only 1. If they have different surface areas, keep both of them.
>
> - Take 12 more cubes. Build a structure with a different surface area.
>
> - Record this new structure and its surface area. Compare its surface area with that of the structure(s) you kept. Keep only the structures with the largest and smallest surface areas.
>
> - Continue to build, record, compare, and eliminate until you are convinced that you have found the structures with the smallest and largest surface areas.

The Bigger Picture

Thinking and Sharing

Invite the pair who thinks they have found the structure with the smallest surface area to display it and explain how they found the surface area. Ask if anyone else has found a different structure with the same or smaller surface area and display it. Repeat the process for the structure with largest surface area. Display all the structures with the largest area.

Use prompts like these to promote class discussion:

- What did you notice as you built your structures?
- Do you think a structure with an even smaller surface area can be made? a larger surface area? Explain.
- How are the structures with the smaller surface areas like the ones with the larger surface areas? How are they different?
- What other surface areas did you find? What patterns did you notice?

Writing

Present children with this scenario: A toy manufacturer needs to design a box for shipping its new product line—GLOP!—to thousands of toy stores. GLOP! is packaged in a plastic cube that measures 3″ on a side. The manufacturer would like to put 24 of these cubes in every shipping box. Ask children to design a box that will use a minimum of cardboard, describe its dimensions, and explain to the manufacturer why this box would be the least expensive choice of packaging for 24 cubes.

Extending the Activity

1. Create a class chart that has 10 columns labeled from left to right with the 10 possible surface areas: 32, 34, 36, 38, 40, 42, 44, 46, 48, 50.

Teacher Talk

Where's the Mathematics?

This activity helps children make a visual and numerical connection between three-dimensional structures (polyhedra) and their two-dimensional surfaces (polygons). As they create different Snap Cube structures, children gain experience in finding surface area. They also learn that different arrangements of the same number of cubes do not necessarily produce structures with different surface areas.

With 12 cubes, the smallest possible surface area is 32 and the largest is 50. Children are often surprised to see that there is only one structure—the 2 x 3 x 2 rectangular prism—that has the minimum surface area of 32, whereas many structures have the maximum of 50. In fact, it is possible to build at least one structure that has an even surface area between these two numbers.

Here are some possible structures children may come up with.

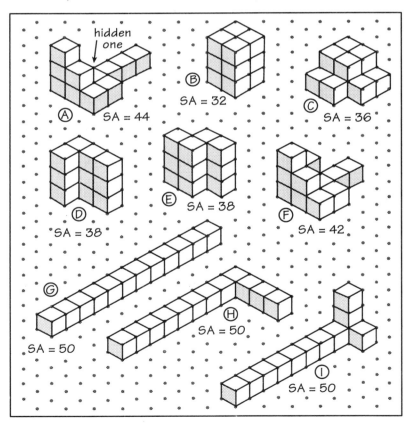

Encourage children to explain how and why surface area changes—or does not change—as they rearrange cubes. For example, moving three cubes in

Have children cut apart and post their isometric recordings. Compare and discuss the postings.

2. Ask children to repeat the activity with 16 or 24 Snap Cubes.

structure G (above) results in structure H. Yet, the surface area remains unchanged. Although one new cube face is exposed at the end of the nine cubes, a previously exposed cube face is covered up by the "ell."

Since counting cube faces takes a long time and it is easy to lose track, children often try to devise shortcuts for figuring surface area. One shortcut is to "walk around" the structure by counting the visible faces from each of the six points of view (top, bottom, front, back, left side, right side) and adding these six numbers.

Another shortcut is to start with a structure and keep track of the faces that appear and disappear as cubes are moved. A child might describe the shortcut in going from structure A to structure F this way: "I started with A which had a surface area of 44. I removed the cube at the end of the tail and put it over the hidden cube to create F. By removing the end cube, 5 faces disappear at the same time that 1 new face appears. That brings the surface area down to 40. When I cover the hidden cube, 2 faces are lost and 4 are added. That brings the surface area up to 42. So structure F has a surface area of 42."

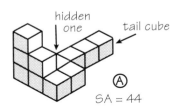
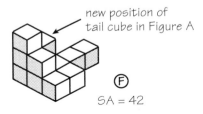

There are several ways to explain why the surface area is always even. To begin, the front and back of a structure always have the same surface area, as do the left and right sides and the top and bottom. Since the surface areas of the six views occur in pairs, the sum would have to be even. Another explanation starts with the surface area of one cube. A single cube has a surface area of 6. As soon as a second cube is joined to the first, each loses one cube face at the join. So the two joined cubes have a total surface area of 12 – 2 or 10. Adding another cube to the structure causes another face to be covered, and 5 more to be added. Thus, the three joined cubes have a surface area of 10 – 1 + 5 or 14.

The class discussion helps children to generalize: When you want the greatest surface area for a given volume, you create long structures such as a 1 x 1 x 12 prism. On the other hand, if you wish to minimize surface area, you should create a compact, cube-like structure, such as a 3 x 2 x 2.

TRIANGULAR NUMBER SEQUENCE

- Triangular numbers
- Pattern recognition
- Growth patterns

Getting Ready

What You'll Need

Snap Cubes, about 65 per pair

Calculators, 1 per pair

Snap Cube grid paper, page 91 (optional)

Crayons (optional)

Overhead Snap Cubes and/or Snap Cube grid paper transparency (optional)

Overview

Using Snap Cubes, children build staircase models of triangular numbers. They record data about each staircase, look for patterns, and make conjectures. In this activity, children have the opportunity to:

- ◆ represent a numerical sequence geometrically
- ◆ collect and analyze data
- ◆ learn about a predictable growth pattern
- ◆ use patterns to make predictions

The Activity

Introducing

- ◆ Display one Snap Cube. Identify the faces of the cube as the top, bottom, right, left, front, and back.

- ◆ Tell children that you are going to build a staircase by adding cubes of a different color to the top and right sides of the cube. Add the cubes so that your staircase looks like the one at the right.

- ◆ Ask children to predict what the staircase will look like if you again add cubes to the top and right sides of the exposed Snap Cubes.

- ◆ Have children share their predictions, then add the cubes.

- ◆ Display the new staircase, pointing out that it has a total of six cubes.

- ◆ Explain that since each staircase you make looks like a triangle, the number of cubes they contain—1, 3, and 6—are called *triangular* numbers.

On Their Own

Is there a way to know in advance the number of Snap Cubes you would need and how to connect them in order to build a staircase of any size?

- Work with a partner building staircases that look like these:

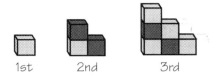

1st   2nd   3rd

- Keep track of the number of cubes you add each time, the total number of cubes in each staircase, and the patterns you find.

- Predict what the 4th staircase will look like, then build it.

- Build staircases until you can use your findings to describe, in detail, a 100-step staircase without building it.

The Bigger Picture

Thinking and Sharing

Create a class chart with three columns. Label the first column *Step Number,* the second column *Number of Cubes in the Step,* and the third column *Total Number of Cubes.* Have children fill in the chart and discuss the data.

Use prompts such as these to promote class discussion:

- What did you notice as you built bigger and bigger staircases?

- What patterns do you notice in the data?

- How many structures did you need to build before you could make predictions about the 100-step staircase? Why?

- How did you find the number of cubes needed for a 100-step staircase?

- How is a 100-step staircase different from a 99-step staircase? from a 101-step staircase?

Writing

Ask children to explain to a grocery clerk how many cans of pineapple chunks he would need to make a triangular display of cans that has at least fifteen cans in the bottom row.

Extending the Activity

1. Challenge children to find how many steps could be built by using 300 cubes.

This activity is the first of a four-lesson sequence and can be followed by the lessons "Squares and Staircases," "Greek Cross Numbers," and "Pyramid Numbers."

Where's the Mathematics?

In this activity, children predict, test, and conjecture. They also informally learn about *functions*, an algebraic relationship between pairs of numbers.

Step Number	Number of Cubes in the Step	Total Number of Cubes in the Staircase
1	1	1
2	2	3
3	3	6
4	4	10
5	5	15
6	6	21
7	7	28
8	8	36
9	9	45
10	10	55

The class chart above shows that the number of cubes in each step corresponds to the step number. To extend the data in the third column, some children will add the previous entry in column 3 to the diagonal entry in column 2.

Step Number	Number of Cubes in the Step	Total Number of Cubes in the Staircase
1	1	1
2	2	3
3	3	6

Others will add as many second-column entries as they need.

Step Number	Number of Cubes in the Step	Total Number of Cubes in the Staircase
1	1	1
2	2	3
3	3	6

Some children may notice a shortcut when adding up long columns of consecutive numbers. They pair numbers that have the same sum, then count the pairs and multiply that number by the sum. In the example shown, there are five pairs whose sum is 12.

2. Have children graph their data. On one graph, the numbers along the horizontal axis can represent the "Step Number" and the numbers along the vertical axis can represent the "Number of Cubes in the Step." On a second graph, change the vertical axis so it represents "Total Number of Cubes." Have children compare their graphs.

Thus, the number of cubes in the eleventh staircase may be found by multiplying 5 times 12 and adding 6.

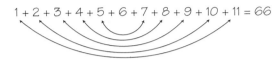

Children can visualize this shortcut by building a staircase, then rearranging the rows as shown below.
Based on the patterns they found, children may describe the 100-step staircase as the sum of 1 to 100. Others may reason like this: A 100-step

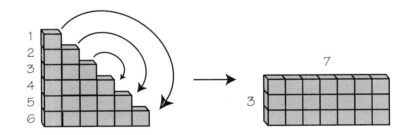

staircase has 100 steps. The last step has 100 cubes whereas the first has 1 cube; the next-to-last step has 99 steps whereas the second step has 2 cubes. Pairing the remaining steps produces 50 pairs, each with a total of 101. The 100-step staircase, therefore, requires 5,051 Snap Cubes.

Still others may focus on the difference pattern found in the numbers in the third column of the class chart—1, 3, 6, 10, 15, and so on. The differences between adjacent pairs are 2, 3, 4, 5, and so on. With the help of a calculator, children can continue adding consecutive numbers until they reach 5,051.

Triangular numbers are often represented by an array of dots. The dots are arranged either as right triangles or as equilateral triangles.

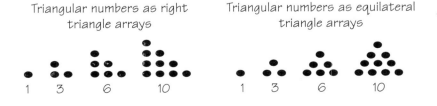

Triangular numbers as right triangle arrays

Triangular numbers as equilateral triangle arrays

WHAT'S THE CHANCE?

- Organizing data
- Interpreting data

Getting Ready

What You'll Need

Snap cubes, 36 per pair

Dice, 2 of different colors per pair

What's the Chance? board, page 92

What's the Chance? board transparency (optional)

Overview

Children use Snap Cubes to track the results of multiple rolls of two dice. In this activity, children have the opportunity to:

- ◆ investigate the relationship between theoretical and experimental probability
- ◆ collect and analyze data
- ◆ discover that the larger the sample, the closer the results will be to a theoretical model

The Activity

Introducing

- ◆ Show children the *What's the Chance?* board and a pair of dice. Explain that the numbers across the top of the board represent one die and the numbers on the side represent the die of a different color.
- ◆ Roll the dice and put a Snap Cube on the corresponding space on the board. Point out that order matters. For example, show by placing cubes on the board that a roll of a red 5 and a white 1 is different from a roll of a red 1 and a white 5.
- ◆ Have children practice rolling the dice and placing cubes on the board to be sure that they understand how to place the cubes properly.

On Their Own

> ### What does a What's the Chance? board look like after 36 rolls of the dice?
>
> - Work with a partner. One partner rolls the dice. The other partner places a Snap Cube on the space that corresponds to the sum rolled.
>
> - Before you start rolling the dice, predict what the board will look like after 36 rolls of the dice.
>
> - Now roll the dice 36 times. If a result happens more than once, stack cubes on top of one another on that space.
>
> - After you have rolled the dice 36 times, count how many numbers are covered by 0 cubes, 1 cube, 2 cubes, 3 cubes, and 4 or more cubes. Record.
>
> - Compare your results to the prediction you made.
>
> - Play 3 rounds. Switch rolls each time.

The Bigger Picture

Thinking and Sharing

Create a large class chart like the one shown below. Have pairs of children form small groups, combine their results, and post their data on the class chart. Ask children to compare their totals to the class totals.

	Number of cells covered by:					Totals
	0 cubes	1 cube	2 cubes	3 cubes	4 or more cubes	
Group 1 Totals	41	36	23	6	2	108
Group 2 Totals						
Group 3 Totals						

Use prompts such as these to promote class discussion:

- Did you completely cover your board after each round? Did you have any spaces that contained more than four Snap Cubes? that contained no Snap Cubes?

- Did your results surprise you? Why or why not?

- How did your results compare to the class totals?

- Which space seems to be covered more often than the others? Why?

- Which space seems to be covered least often? Why?

Extending the Activity

1. Ask children to predict how many times they would have to roll the dice in order to cover every space on the board at least once. Ask them to explain their predictions.

Teacher Talk

Where's the Mathematics?

Children are very likely to predict that every space on the board will be covered or that there will be very few uncovered spaces. Once they generate their charts, they are usually surprised to find that about ⅓ or more of the board is left uncovered in their individual samples. This chart shows typical results of three rounds. In each of these rounds (samples), the number of spaces uncovered accounts for about ⅓ ($^{13}/_{36}$, $^{16}/_{36}$, and $^{12}/_{36}$) of the total spaces on the board.

	Number of cells covered by:					
	0 cubes	1 cube	2 cubes	3 cubes	4 or more cubes	Totals
Round 1	13	12	9	2	0	36
Round 2	16	11	4	3	2	36
Round 3	12	13	10	1	0	36
Total	41	36	23	6	2	108

In a class of 30 children where each pair did the experiment three times, the class chart would show results for 45 samples. Forty-five samples may or may not be sufficient to come up with a case in which all spaces on the board get covered. However, with more and more rolls (beyond the 36 specified in the activity), all squares will eventually be covered.

One way to help children to understand what is happening in this activity is to compare it to an experiment with which they are probably familiar: rolling one die. In this experiment, theory says that in six rolls, a 1 should appear once, a 2 should appear once, and so on. In reality, it is rare for each number to appear once in any six consecutive rolls. Yet, if the die is

2. Have children predict what the class chart would look like if more samples were added. Then have them continue to sample (play rounds of *What's the Chance?*) over the next several days and add the results to the chart, or pool your class's results with those of other classes in the school and compare the results to their predictions.

rolled repeatedly—20, 30, 40, or more times—the results would "even out," that is, each number would appear about the same number of times. You may wish to have the class actually do the experiment, collect the data, and note how the outcomes even out.

In *What's the Chance?*, there are 36 outcomes of the two color combinations. For example, six 7's could occur by rolling six different combinations (1,6), (2,5), (3,4), (4,3), (5,2), and (6,1) or by rolling only two different combinations repeatedly (1,6), (1,6), (1,6), (4,3), (4,3), (1,6). In the first scenario, every 7 on the *What's the Chance?* board would be covered with one Snap Cube. In the second scenario, only two 7's would be covered—the 7 space at the top right would have 4 cubes, the 7 space three over and four down would have 2 cubes, and the rest of the 7 spaces would be uncovered. In *What's the Chance?*, *how* each number is rolled in each scenario matters, not simply *what* number was rolled.

This might be a good time to introduce symbolism if children are not already familiar with it. The probability of rolling a red 6 and a white 1 is 1 out of 36. Do several examples with the class focusing on the chart so that they can see why 1 out of 36 makes sense. Show them how mathematicians write ordered pairs (6,1) and that the probability of any pair is $\frac{1}{36}$ and is denoted like this: $P(6,1) = \frac{1}{36}$. The order of the numbers in the ordered pair depends on what the class has decided. The order in one class might be (red die first, white die second). In another class, it might be (white die first, red die second).

Ask children to consider the probability of getting a 7. Looking at the chart, there are 6 different squares marked 7. Therefore, $P(7) = \frac{6}{36}$ or $\frac{1}{6}$.

	•	••	•••	::	:::	::::
•	2	3	4	5	6	7
••	3	4	5	6	7	8
•••	4	5	6	7	8	9
::	5	6	7	8	9	10
:::	6	7	8	9	10	11
::::	7	8	9	10	11	12

SNAP CUBE WRITING PAPER